GLIMPSES OF

INDIAN NATIONAL CONGRESS

FROM INCEPTION TO
ATTAINMENT OF FREEDOM
1885 –1947

MAHATMA GANDHI
FATHER OF THE NATION

GLIMPSES OF INDIAN NATIONAL CONGRESS

FROM INCEPTION TO ATTAINMENT OF FREEDOM 1885 –1947

T.N. KUNDRA

Regency Publications
New Delhi

ISBN 81-86030-12-3

Published by Regency Publications, 20/36-G, Old Market, West Patel Nagar, New Delhi 110 008 and printed at Radiant Printers, New Delhi 110 008. Phones: 571 3968, 578 3571.

"Truth is God"

ANAND T. HINGORANI
Editor-Publisher: *"GANDHI SERIES"*

C/18-D, Munirka
New Delhi-110067
Phone: 66 74 98
Dated December 16, 1995

FOREWORD

Shri T.N. Kundra is quite a well-known figure in Delhi, especially in the Congress circles. Being a Congressman and a veteran Freedom Fighter himself, and having served as an Honorary Secretary/Convener of the Freedom Fighters' Relief Committee of the Delhi Administration for over 22 years, he has naturally come to enjoy a very close rapport with freedom fighters of all kinds. Incidentally, this also provided him with a splendid opportunity for mutual exchange of views and experiences of those good old times when the Indian National Congress, under the divinely-inspired leadership of Mahatma Gandhi, and the most dynamic and charismatic personality of Jawaharlal Nehru and several other Congress stalwarts, carried on the glorious freedom struggle against the British rule. This struggle was most unique and unparalleled in the entire history of mankind, based as it was not on any physical or military might, but on sheer moral and spiritual forces—on Gandhiji's twin principles of Truth and Non-violence.

After a long and arduous fight and undergoing all sorts of sufferings and sacrifices, when our nation finally achieved its goal of Complete Independence in 1947, India's prestige immediately went up sky-high amongst all the nations of the world, and Mahatma Gandhi was acclaimed by the whole of humanity as an Apostle of Peace and Love.

Kundraji has really done a great service by bringing out this handy beautiful book, containing a bird's-eye view of the history of our now 110-year old political organization—the Indian National Congress—from its inception in 1885 to the attainment of freedom in 1947. And, as the book does not embody full and comprehensive history, he has, therefore, rightly titled it as The Glimpses of Indian National Congress. In presenting these glimpses in a book form, Kundraji's idea was to acquaint the modern generation, particularly the youth of our country who have merely heard the name of the Congress, but know not how and when it came into being, and what tremendous efforts it had put forth in awakening our teeming millions from their deep slumber of slavery, and infusing in them the spirit of nationalism and resistance to the alien rule to the point of active non-violent revolution, and eventually winning Swaraj which, in the words of Lokmanya Tilak, was our birthright.

One most laudable feature of this very interesting and informative book is that it contains pithy extracts from the addresses delivered at the annual Congress Sessions by the most eminent personalities of the day who presided over them. These valuable and discreetly selected quotations from the Presidential speeches are extremely inspiring, and these are star-marked so as to easily draw the reader's attention to them. I think if one were to read these extracts only, he would come to know all about the growth of the Congress from being an evolutionary body at the start of its career in 1885, to becoming a revolutionary one in 1929, when it proudly and defiantly declared, at the Lahore Congress Session in December, *Purna Swaraj* (Complete Independence) as its goal for attainment.

I am personally thankful to Kundraji for including these precious extracts in his book which, as I went on reading at this old age of 88, once again aroused in me the spirit of my youthful days when at the age of 22, having chucked up my law studies, I attended that historic Lahore Congress Session in December 1929, and, at the invitation of Gandhiji, I joined his Sabarmati Ashram in January 1930 and, soon thereafter, on March 12, I participated in his famous Dandi March to break the Salt Laws and also in all his subsequent *Satyagraha* movements. Indeed, it gave me immense joy to re-live those stirring times when one felt sanctified in offering the highest sacrifice at the altar of our beloved Motherland's freedom.

The book is replete with many other equally fascinating features, which the reader would do well to go through if he wishes to be an enlightened citizen of India. This book eminently deserves to be placed in every school, college, university and public library in our country, and I hope the authorities concerned will not fail to realize its intrinsic worth and value.

My sincere congratulations to Kundraji on the production of this most valuable book.

C-18/D, Munirka,
New Delhi 110 067
(125 Birth Anniversary of
Mahatma Gandhi)

Anand T. Hingorani

(ANAND T. HINGORANI)
Editor Publisher: "*Gandhi Series*"

PREFACE

"CONGRESS IS A DIVINE MISSION"
—*Sir Surendra Nath Banerjee, 1902.*

It is heartening that in the Centenary Year of the Indian National Congress, a number of excellent volumes by eminent writers, journalists and historians have come up enabling, thereby, better appraisals of men and events, which dominated the freedom struggle initiated by the Indian National Congress. This small monograph, which I have produced, may not appreciably add to the vast literary and historical treasure already available on this theme. Yet, it might be useful to young readers (for whom it is especially intended), who may not be well acquainted with the nostalgic saga of heroism, trials and tribulations which the Indian National Congress had to encounter in its memorable struggle against the Imperial rulers, who were made to abdicate power and transfer sovereignty to our people. As a Congressman, who had the privilege of having participated in this great national crusade, I have watched the ebbs and flows of this historic process. I have also had frequent occasions to exchange thoughts on the subject with many of my fellow freedom fighters, the actual participants, in my capacity as the Honorary Secretary/Convenor of the Freedom Fighters Relief Committee of Delhi Administration for over 22 years. All this has greatly helped me in the preparation of this condensed volume.

The theme is of perennial interest to posterity. Not even prolix volumes can do adequate justice to it. I am, therefore, conscious of my limitation. Moreover, a small book for young readers will have served its utility only if glimpses of this historic national struggle can be portrayed.

The Congress successfully withstood the storm against the mighty British repressive regime. Legions of our countrymen faced deprivation of life and property. Hundreds courted jail or became victims of lathi charge, police firing and other oppressive measures. But the men and the women, who participated in this patriotic upsurge, had an extraordinary inner strength, the will to conquer all obstacles to the freedom of the country, a grim determination to suffer and conquer and they did finally succeed in the liquidation of the British Empire in South Asia in 1947. Lesser stalwarts could not have enabled the Congress to weather the storm !.

This, indeed, was the crown of glory for the Congress. It was, more so, an epitaph on the most brilliant chapter of the imperial history of Great Britain, which after the loss of India, was reduced to a mediocre power. The Congress struggled and released forces of nationalism on a massive scale. This, supplemented by other revolutionary factors, such as the I.N.A., the economic insolvency of Britain as a result of the Second World War, incapacitated Britain to retain the Indian Dominion any longer. The freedom of India opened flood gates for the exit of colonial powers elsewhere also.

When the last British troops left our shores, the world was never the same again. It was a great moment; the greatest phenomenon in world history in the twentieth century and a splendid occasion ! But, the price exacted was no smaller. India was partitioned, as the erstwhile Imperial rulers were able to take advantage of the communal mistrust they had deliberately pampered. The pangs of separation have not as yet subsided. After India became free on the 15th of August, 1947, the Congress faced the challenging task of building up a new Nation. It shouldered this responsibility in an admirable way. As the dominant party, it gave a Constitution to India based on the civilised principles of equality and social justice, democracy and socialism. Save for a brief interruption of five years (1977–1980 and 1990–1991), the Congress being the dominant repository of authority has gone a long way in transforming India into a forward looking modern nation busy in developing science, high technology, agriculture and industry to rid its teeming millions of poverty and ignorance.

Besides, the Congress is a significant, international force which has guided the Indian Government, sponsored by its electoral victories, in its constant support to non-alignment and to the freedom struggles against the colonial and exploitative forces of weaker nations on a global scale. Under the Congress Rule, India has successfully foiled foreign invasions, including several wars enforced by Pakistan. In 1971, under Smt. Indira Gandhi's leadership, a convincing victory over Pakistan resulted in the birth of Bangladesh. But, an emerging nation has to face obstacles in its development. The Congress has to act, therefore, beyond the normal frontiers of a political party and to work hard to consolidate the freedom of India, as well as to make it a prosperous and just society.

Looking retrospectively, particular mention must be made of the address of 'Mahamana' Pt. Madan Mohan Malviya at the Delhi Congress of 1918, which reflected his inexpressible sorrow and shame at the state to which our country had fallen to argue with the British Rulers for our capacity for a limited measure of autonomy. This inspired me to study addresses of the Congress Presidents, from the birth of the Congress till the attainment of freedom. I have selected some extracts which show how steadily this great organisation came to be transformed from a debating club of highly educated Indians expressing loyalty to the British Crown, demanding certain concessions, enjoying finest oratory and hospitality of the Governors and Governor Generals to an organisation based on the support of the masses, challenging thereby, the mighty British Power for removing the yoke of slavery.

The first journey of this great organisation ended on 15th August, 1947 only to embark on the second—to redeem its pledge to make India a strong, prosperous, socialist country, to wipe out tear from every eye and also to be the champion of those who were still in bondage, as 'Freedom' and 'Slavery' cannot co-exist.

In compiling this book, I have drawn heavily on several publications such as 'Living an Era' by D.P. Mishra, Ex. Chief Minister, Madhya Pradesh, 'Mahatma' by D.G. Tendulkar,

'Sixty Years of Congress', 'Pilgrim's Progress' by my friend and colleague Shri Prabodh Chandra, former Speaker and Minister of Punjab, and 'Road to Freedom' by Comrade Ram Chandra, B.A. (National) besides a host of other noted writers. I express my sincere gratitude to the concerned authors and publishers.

I have no words to express my love and regards for Dr. Dharmendra Nath for his encouragement to write; without his encouragement I would not have dared to do so. My thanks are also due to Shri B.D. Sharma for his invaluable suggestions and guidance.

In case this attempt of mine which provides only glimpses of the odyssey of this great organisation, enthuses the readers to study history of the Freedom Movement and the Congress, and to be dedicated to the service of the nation, I would feel amply rewarded.

I will like to close on a hopeful note. In this context, may I quote the inimitable words of our late Prime Minister, Smt. Indira Gandhi, expressed in a message to Freedom Fighters:

> "By participating in a cause larger than himself, every Indian grew in stature. The darkness of oppression was illuminated by great intellects, poets, scientists, indeed people of all professions were one in a great objective—the resurgence of the Nation. Ultimately success was achieved by our people, the countless men and women who served our cause by their numbers, no less by their dedication. We had faith that people who moved with dignity and courage could not be cowed and that India awakened could not again be subdued."

I dedicate this book to freedom fighters and patriots whose sacrifices can never be adequately evaluated.

VANDE MATRAM

Delhi, Dated October 2, 1995 T.N. KUNDRA

CONTENTS

1

BIRTH OF THE CONGRESS— ITS GENESIS

"There is no legitimacy on earth, but in a government which is the choice of the nation."

— *Joseph Bonaparte*

The failure of the 1st War of Independence of 1857 left bitterness on both sides. After that, there was no sign of political activity for a decade or so. From 1870 Indian Press specially 'Amrit Bazar Patrika' of Calcutta and Reformist leaders like Swami Dayanand, Raja Ram Mohan Roy, Swami Vivekanand and others created a spirit of self respect among Indians. Indian Nationalism entered a new phase of development. Lives of Garibaldi, Mazzini etc., which were translated in Indian languages infused the spirit of Nationalism. Western education too helped us to move in this direction. There was a demand from all quarters for equality. During the Viceroyalty of Lord Ripon a bill (well known as Ilbert Bill) was introduced by Ilbert, putting Europeans and Indians on equal footing in criminal proceedings. This was vehemently opposed by British officers and merchants. This created a counter resentment among Indians. Lord Ripon was recalled under the pressure of British civil servants and business tycoons in India. 'Amrit Bazar Patrika' wrote, "India is a land where it is impossible for a man like Ripon to stay."

British in India, had excluded Indians from responsible posts in the administrative hierarchy. After 1833, the Company had ceased to be a trading corporation and had become the dominant ruling power. The lease granted to it by the Royal Charter in 1833 was to expire in 1853 and the question

A.O. HUME
FOUNDER OF THE CONGRESS

of renewal of the charter came up. The small Indian elite which had received Western education felt that it was time to challenge the right of the British East India Company to govern India, under a system no longer adequate. They particularly resented exclusion of Indians from higher posts, though a specific provision existed in the Act of 1833 that "No native of India or natural born subject therein should be disqualified from office by reason only of religion, place of birth, descent or colour." The British public took little interest in the welfare of subject India, but the Indian intelligentsia could not ignore their exclusion contrary to the statute, from the services. They were anxious to ventilate these and other public grievances. On August 26, 1852, the citizens of Bombay organised a meeting in the premises of Elphinston Institution and a political Association namely 'The Bombay Association' was formed under the leadership of the grand old man of Bombay Dadabhai Naoroji.

A similar organisation was formed in Madras, namely "The East India Association", which was inaugurated on December 1, 1866, in collaboration with a Committee of retired British Officers.

Its membership was open to all who might be interested in the welfare of India. The first President of the said Association was Calcutta-born Lord Lyveden, son of Robert Smith, the Advocate General of Bengal. A large number of eminent British politicians, ex-governors and ex-officials resident in England had joined this Association. Dadabhai Naoroji was, to begin with, only a member of the Committee of this Association. Later, he became its Secretary.

At the first gathering of this Committee (residents of England) of the East India Association which was held on May 2, 1867, Dadabhai read a paper on 'England's Duties to India.' Later important papers ventilating India's grievances to the British public were read at its gathering by eminent persons, both Indian and British.

In 1883, Shri Tarapando Banerjee proposed establishment of a fund to maintain a permanent representative in London to enlighten Englishmen regarding the aspirations and feelings of Indians. Need of an organisation representing all parts of the country was discussed in 1884 in Madras by the delegates to the Annual Convention of Theosophical Society. Proclamation of the British Queen on the assumption of the governance of India by the Crown that "Our subjects of whatever race or creed be freely and impartially admitted to the offices in our services" was being thwarted vehemently by the bureaucracy. At that time a noble soul Mr. A.O. Hume—a retired I.C.S. was inspired to intervene with the idea to find out ways and means of directing the impulse of the Indians of which he had alarming evidence, into innocuous channel. Mr. Hume's idea was that of provincial organisations to meet yearly, presided over by the respective Governor to take up political questions to create cordiality between rulers and ruled. Lord Dufferin the Viceroy took great interest in the matter. He was of the opinion that publicmen might not speak their minds in the presence of Governors. Hume addressed a letter to the graduates of Calcutta University asking for fifty men—good and true men of unselfishness, moral courage, self-control and active spirit to join the founders. The concluding portion of that soul-stirring letter is as follows:

- "And if even the leaders of thought are all either such poor creatures or so selfishly wedded to personal concerns that they dare not strike a blow for their country's sake then justly and rightly are they kept down and trampled on, for they deserve nothing better. Every nation secures precisely as good government as it merits. If you, the picked men, the most highly educated of the nation can not, scorning personal ease and selfish objects, make a resolute struggle to secure greater freedom for yourselves and your country, a more impartial administration, a larger share in the management of your affairs, then we, your friends are wrong and our adversaries right, then the Lord Ripon's noble aspirations for your good are fruitless and visionary, then at present at any rate all hopes of progress are at an end and India truly neither desires nor deserves any better Government than she enjoys."

This letter created a stir and men of goodwill stirred with the spirits of national idealism, and Indian National Congress was born.

It was decided to hold the first session of the Indian National Congress at Poona. Due to outbreak of plague in Poona, it was finally held in December, 1885 in Bombay. Now let us have a glimpse of the journey of this great organisation from year to year, till it achieved complete Independence from foreign yoke in 1947.

See annexure showing the year, locale and names and Presidents of the Indian National Congress from its inception to the year 1946 at the end of the book.

2

THE EARLY PHASE

FIRST SESSION—1885 AT BOMBAY

W.C. BONNERJEE

Mr. W.C. Bonnerjee of Calcutta presided over the session which was attended by only 72 delegates. The aims and objects of the Congress were defined as under:

(a) The promotion of the personal intimacy, and friendship amongst all the more earnest workers in our country's cause in various parts of the Empire.

(b) The eradication, by direct friendly personal, intercourse of all possible race, creed, or provincial prejudices amongst all lovers of our country and the fuller developments and consolidation of those sentiments of national unity that had their origin in their beloved Lord Ripon's ever memorable reign.

(c) The authoritative record after this has been carefully elicited by the fullest discussion of the matured opinions of the educated classes in India, on some of the more important and pressing of the social questions of the day.

(d) The determination of the lines upon and methods by which during the next twelve months it is desirable for native politicians to labour in the public interest.

The President in his address emphasized the importance and comprehensiveness of the Congress and claimed it as being representative of whole of India. He further said:

- "Our desire to be governed according to the ideas of Government prevalent in Europe, was in a way incompatible with our thorough loyalty to the British Government. All we desired was that the basis of the Government should be widened and that the people should have their proper and legitimate share in it."

Among other topics, it passed a resolution for the appointment of a Royal Commission to enquire into the working of the Constitution of India.

SECOND SESSION—1886 AT CALCUTTA

DADABHAI NAOROJI

It was presided over by Bombay's grand old man Dadabhai Naoroji (who also presided the sessions of 1893 and 1906). It goes to his credit that this session defined the goal of India a Swaraj (Self Government). Among the delegates were Pt. Madan Mohan Malviya, Surendra Nath Banerjee etc. Among resolutions there was a demand for having 50% elected members in the Councils. It also opposed the powers of Sessions Judges and High Court Judges of setting aside the verdicts of juries. Viceroy Lord Dufferin invited delegates to his garden party as distinguished visitors.

In his Presidential address Dadabhai said:

- "National Congress must confine itself to questions in which entire nation has a direct participation and it must leave the adjustment of social reforms and other class questions to class congresses".

- "The assemblage of such a Congress is an event of the utmost importance in Indian History. Is this Congress a nursery for sedition and rebellion against the British Government, or it is another stone in the foundation of the stability of the Government ?"

THIRD SESSION—1887 AT MADRAS

Justice Badruddin Tyabji presided and 607 delegates attended. One delegate Mr. Eardley Norton in his speech said:

- "If it be sedition to rebel against all wrongs, if it be sedition to insist that people should have a fair share in the administration of their own country and affairs, if it be sedition to resist class tyranny to raise any voice against oppression, to mutiny against injustice, to insist upon a hearing before sentence, to uphold the liberties of the individual, to vindicate our common right to gradual but ever advancing reforms, if this be sedition I am rightly glad to be called a seditionist and doubly eye, trebly glad when I look around me to know, and feel, that I am ranked as one, among such a magnificent array of seditionists."

In his Presidential address Mr. Badruddin Tyabji dwelled upon the representative character of Congress. He failed to understand why Muslims should not work shoulder to shoulder with their fellow countrymen for the common benefit of all.

Governor of Madras Lord Connemara attended the reception given by Mr. Norton and received the delegates at Government House.

3

THE DEVELOPING PHASE

FOURTH SESSION—1888 AT ALLAHABAD

GEORGE YULE

A Britisher Mr. George Yule presided over this session. Whereas Congress was growing in strength, opposition from Sir Auckland Colvin and Sir Syed Ahmed also gained strength. Sir Syed Ahmed Khan gave a call to his co-religionists to keep away from the Congress and the Anglo-Muslim Defence Association was formed. This opposition had an opposite effect and the session of the Congress that year was more successful than those of the previous years. One Sheikh Raza Hussain produced a Fatwa from religious leaders supporting the Congress. Mr. Yule in his presidential address said:

- "We desire no sudden snapping of existing ties. We ask only loosening of the bonds. All movements of the nature of Congress was through several phases as they run their course. The first is one of ridicule. That is followed, as movement progresses by one of abuse which is generally succeeded by partial concession, and misapprehension of aim, accompanied by warnings against taking a big jump into the unknown. The final stage of all is a substantial adoption of the object of the movement, with some expression of the surprise that it was not adopted before. These various phases overlap each other but between the first and last is a complete distinction."

Inspite of several obstacles placed by Sir Auckland in the way of the Reception Committee more than 1200 delegates attended the session. For the first time delegates (20) from Delhi participated in the Congress Session.

The session demanded an enquiry into the police adminstration. It also demanded facilities for technical education and industrial enterprises.

FIFTH SESSION—1889 AT BOMBAY

It was presided over by Sir William Wedderburn, who retired from Indian Civil Service in 1887. He, in his presidential address said:

- "I have been in the service of the people of India and have eaten their salt and I hope to devote to their service what still remains to me of active life."

WILLIAM WEDDERBURN

The main feature of this session was the presence of Mr. Charles Bradlaugh, a member of British Parliament. He introduced a Bill based on the scheme submitted by the Congress in the House of Commons in 1890, but British Government in order to forestall it, introduced a bill of its own.

In reply to an address presented by the Congress to Mr. Bradlaugh, he said:

- "For whom should I work, if not for the people? Born of the people, trusted by the people, I will DIE for the people, and I know no geographical or race limitations."

A Committee consisting of M/s Pherozeshah Mehta, Surendra Nath Banerjee, W.C. Bonnerjee and five Englishmen was appointed to conduct campaign in England.

Gopal Krishna Gokhale joined the Congress.

SIXTH SESSION—1890 AT CALCUTTA

This session was presided over by Sir Pherozeshah Mehta. In his presidential address he said:

- "To my mind a Parsi is a true Parsi, a Mohammedan or a Hindu is a better Mohammedan or Hindu, the more he is attached to the land which gave him birth, the more he is bound in brotherly relations and attached to all the children of the soil."

PHEROZESHAH MEHTA

Secretary to the Governor of Bengal returned the invitation cards sent by the Reception Committee saying that as per Government of India's order presence of Government servants was prohibited in such meetings.

SEVENTH SESSION—1891 AT NAGPUR

This session was presided over by Mr. P. Ananda Charlu—a shining light of South India for two decades. In his stirring address he demanded establishment of Military Colleges and relaxation in Arms Act. Congress reiterated its conviction that India could not be governed well until the people were allowed through their elected representatives a potential voice in the legislature. He described Indian Council "as the oligarchy of fossilised Indian Administrators who were superannuated for service in India."

EIGHTH SESSION—1892 AT ALLAHABAD

This session was presided over by Mr. W.C. Bonnerjee. He in his address defended the decision of the Congress not to involve itself into social questions. The main feature of the session was the speech of grand old man of Punjab, Lala Murli Dhar, who said:

- "You ! you, it seems, are content to join with those accursed monsters in battening on the hearts' blood of your brethren (Cries of 'no' 'no'). I say, yes, look round, what are these chandeliers and lamps, and European made chairs, and tables and smart clothes, and hats, and English coats, the bonnets, and frocks, and silver mounted canes, and all the luxurious fittings of your houses but trophies of Indian's misery, monuments of misery, monuments of Indian's starvation. Every rupee you have spent on Europe-made articles is a rupee of which you have robbed your poor brethren, honest handicraftsmen who can now no longer earn a living. Of course, it was a pure philanthropy which flooded India with English-made goods and, surely and slowly, killed out every indigenous industry, fine philanthropy which, to facilitate this, repeated the import duties and flung away three crores a year of a revenue, which the rich paid, and to balance this wicked sacrifices raised the Salt Tax which the poor pay, which is now pressing factory regulations on us to kill, if possible, the one tiny new industrial departure India could boast of. Oh yes ! it is all philanthropy but the result is that you brethren are starving. Not 30 years ago, wheat was available at the rate of 1½ maunds per rupee, and gram 2 maunds for a rupee, for our grain was not exported to foreign lands. Now it is six times as dear and six times as hard for the poor to fill their bellies because our philanthropists have conjured up the phantasm of free trade to drain our granaries. Free trade, free play, between these two nations. How I hate the sham: what fair play in trade can there be between impoverished India, and the bloated capitalist England ?"

NINTH SESSION—1893 AT LAHORE

Mr. Dadabhai Naoroji who was elected to British Parliament presided over the session. It was the first session in Punjab which was then considered politically a backward province, because of the Muslim majority who kept themselves away from the Congress. In this session economic issues and political favours for educated classes were in prominence, as financiers in Britain began to regard India as a profitable market for investment than anything else. By this time, Indians, with very few rare exceptions had failed to appreciate the manner in which their country was being utilised for England's benefits and the way in which British Capital was being encouraged, while savings of Indians were allowed to lie idle and were not utilised for great public works which were being built. Pt. Madan Mohan Malviya in a forceful speech said:

- "Where are the weavers ? Where are those men who lived by different industries and manufactures, and where are the manufactures which were sent to Europe in very large quantities year after year ? All that has become a thing of the past. Every one sitting here is clothed in the cloth of British make, and wherever you go, you find British manufactures and British goods staring you in the face. All that is left to the people is to drag out a miserable existence by agricultural operations and make infinitesimal profit out of the little left to them. In the matter of the services, in the matter of trade, our people are not enjoying one-hundredth of the part of the profit and gain which they used to enjoy fifty years ago. How then is it possible for the country to be happy ?"

In his address Dadabhai Naoroji said, "Punjabis are warrior and a manly race and generosity is their marked characteristic."

TENTH SESSION—1894 AT MADRAS

This session was presided over by Mr. Alfred Webb—an Irish member of British Parliament. His visit to India and presiding over the Congress Session was considered as a message of peace and goodwill. He in his speech said:

- "I was nurtured in the conflict against slavery. My country is the world ! My countrymen are all mankind. I am a friend of civil and religious liberty all over the world. I hate tyranny and repression.
  Nothing is more striking in considering the condition of India than its poverty compared with the wealth of the rest of the world. The mean annual income per head in the United Kingdom is above Rs. 500 while in India it is Rs. 20.
  I regret that in India, the expenditure on army is much more than on education."

This session condemned the excise duty levied on cotton manufactured in British India and put on record its firm conviction that in imposing duty, the interest of India have been sacrificed to those of Lancashire. It also demanded the recruitment for higher judiciary from the Bar.

ELEVENTH SESSION—1895 AT POONA

This session was presided over by Surendra Nath Banerjee of Calcutta, editor of 'The Bengali'. Sir Henry Cotton wrote about him, "From Multan to Chittagaon, Surendra Nath Banerjee can, by the power of the tongue, raise a revolt and suppress a rebellion."

In this session Congress demanded a place for Indians in the Executive Council of Madras and Bombay. In his address the President said:

- "I can conceive no higher honour, no loftier trust, no more exalted dignity than that to which you have summoned me to preside over this session. The highest reward for a publicman next to approbation of his own conscience, is the confidence of his fellow countrymen. But great as the honour is, far higher is the responsibility which belongs to it."

TWELFTH SESSION—1896 AT CALCUTTA

This session was presided over by a Muslim Rahmat Ullah Sayani. In his address he said:

- "The origin of the Congress was thus an epoch in the history of the country and with the establishment of a Congress, began a new era in the political history of the country. Keeping aloof from the Congress is not only undesirable but even merits censure."

The session demanded financial independence for the provinces and reorganisation of educational services.

THIRTEENTH SESSION—1897 AT AMRAVATI

This session was presided over by Mr. Sankaran Nair who resigned the membership of the Viceroy's Executive Council to protest against the reactionary and repressive policies of Lord Chelmsford during Martial Law regime. There was plague in Poona in 1896. A Plague Committee under Mr. Rand was appointed. British soldiers searched the houses and misbehaved with ladies. Mr. Rand was murdered by Mr. Chapekar. Lokmanya Bal Gangadhar Tilak was arrested and sentenced to 18 months' imprisonment. Even an appeal in Privy Council was rejected. Repressive policies of the Government increased. Press was gagged.

Conviction of Tilak overshadowed this session. President Sir Sankaran Nair and Sir Surendra Nath Banerjee paid eloquent tributes to Tilak.

In his address the President said:

- "India expects great things from us. The whole civilized world was watching the changes coming over us. Shall we be content to leave India as it is, or shall we go on and do all in our power to lift it to a higher level."

FOURTEENTH SESSION—1898 AT MADRAS

This session was presided over by Mr. Anand Mohan Bose, who was second only to Sir Surendra Nath Banerjee, as an ardent worker and graceful orator. In his presidential address he said:

- "Time has come when if we are to reap the full fruits of our deliberations and to give living force to our resolutions we must have a standing organisation to carry on the work of the Congress from year's beginning to year's end, to carry on the work continuously, steadily, earnestly, sending agents and missionaries to different parts of the country, spreading information, awakening interest, issuing leaflets and pamphlets, educating the public mind, drawing attention to the many wants and grievances of the dumb masses, we must have men wholly devoted to this work, if Congress is not to be a mere three days' affair."

On this suggestion an effort was made to frame Congress Constitution.

This year Mohandas Karamchand Gandhi began his famous agitation in Natal against Natal Law, which was disgraceful to South African Indians. This was the first ever fight against apartheid in modern history.

FIFTEENTH SESSION—1899 AT LUCKNOW

This session was presided over by Mr. Romesh Chandra Dutt, who retired as the Divisional Commissioner of Burdwan from Indian Civil Services in 1897. He was the first Indian who attained the rank of a Divisional Commissioner and had made a high reputation as an Administrator. This earned him companionship of the Indian Empire. For a time he sat in Bengal Legislative Council and served as Professor of Indian History in a University in Great Britain. Gaikwar Sayajirao appointed him as the Dewan of Baroda, where Dutt died on 30th November, 1909.

Dutt was a prolific writer. Among his best work can be cited 'The Ramayan and Mahabharata' which he had condensed and translated in English verse. Lucknow which is reputed for. its cadres of brilliant writers and poets, was a fitting venue for the Presidential peroration of a scholar/nationalist of such renown.

In his address, Dutt condemned the policies of Lord Curzon, the Viceroy of India with regard to expedition to Tibet, severe measures one after another, the Partition of Bengal, etc. He stated in his address:

- "While every self-governing colony was prosperous and happy, India, alone with vast population was suffering from famine which has spread in 1897 over a vast area. Doubts are being expressed if British rule in India is a blessing for the poor cultivators and labourers of India."

Dutt further said:

- "It is immutable law of nature that you cannot permanently secure the welfare of the people if you tie up the hands of the people themselves. It is possible to prevent disasters and deaths from famines, to spread prosperity and contentment and to evoke the zealous and loyal support of a grateful nation only by conceding to the people—in so far is safely possible blessings of self-government."

Congress Constitution was adopted.

A quarrel over the desire of delegates led by Tilak to condemn the administration of Lord Sandhurst (which was opposed by the supporters of the President) was, however, diffused by the withdrawal of Tilak's supporters in the interest of the Organisation.

SIXTEENTH SESSION—1900 AT LAHORE

This session was presided over by Mr. N.G. Chandaverkar. While he was presiding over the session, he received a telegram that he was appointed Judge of Bombay High Court. This shows how public men were allured by the Government.

Due to repressive policy of the Government, this session was a tame affair and was not well attended. In this session Indian Congress Committee was enlarged.

In his address the President said:

- "I draw hope and inspiration from those I see before me. There is something elevating in the remembrance of the fact that you on whose deliberation I have to preside are all earnest men animated by pure love for their country."

What an honour showered on Punjabis ?

SEVENTEENTH SESSION—1901 AT CALCUTTA

This session was presided over by Mr. D.E. Wacha, a Parsi. He was Secretary of the Congress for a number of years. He was one of the relentless critics of the policies and repressive measures of the Government. He is one of those who considered it a religious duty not to miss any Congress session. He in his address said, "While India is poor, it is being ruled at a cost unheard of in any part of the civilized world."

Admissions of Indians into the Police Competition Examination in England and larger employment in the higher ranks of any army was demanded.

Work of the Congress in London was organised. Its paper "India" was placed on firm basis.

EIGHTEENTH SESSION—1902 AT AHMEDABAD

This session was presided over by Shri Surendra Nath Banerjee. In his address he said:

- "We have an undying faith, as strong as ever inspired by a prophet or a priest, that the cause to which we are pledged will triumph over all difficulties, outlive all prejudices, leading us onward and upward, inspiring at each stage a loftier devotion and developing a truer manhood. I believe the Congress is a Divine Mission."

Resolution regarding increase of pounds 7,86,000 per annum in the capitation charges borne by India on account of British forces in India, regarding the recommendations of the Indian Universities Commission, being retrograde, reactionary and inimical to the best interests of the country were adopted.

NINETEENTH SESSION—1903 AT MADRAS

This session was presided over by Mr. Lal Mohan Ghosh of Bengal. He at the age of 30, was a member of a deputation which was sent to England to protest against the Vernacular Press Act and the reduction of age limit to Indian Civil Service Examination. When he made powerful speech in the first public meeting in London, Mr. John Bright—a great orator of England said, "I will not spoil the effect of the magnificent oration we have heard by any feeble words of mine." In the House of Lords Mr. Gladstone said that the Vernacular Press Act was a disgrace to the Government. When Gladstone became Prime Minister of England, Press Act was repealed. Mr. Ghose was known as Political Yogi in England.

In his presidential address he described Coronation Durbar as a "Pompous pageantry to a perishing people." He made an impassioned appeal for educating the masses.

Sh. Ghosh further said:

- "Let us remember that we can never hope to realise our aspirations unless the Congress is fully sensible towards the masses of our people, and shape its policy as to bring them in line with us.
- Young men of India, in you the hopes of our country are centred and I can not bring home to you the responsibilities which rest on you better than this ! Gentlemen ! the fate of India is in your hands."

Resolution was against the proposed Indian Universities Bill and Official Secret Bill.

TWENTIETH SESSION—1904 AT BOMBAY

This session was presided over by Sir Henry Cotton—an I.C.S. man—Chief Commissioner of Assam, who after retirement, had joined the Congress. Sir Cotton was denied Lt. Governorship of Bengal for his advocacy for the cause of coolies. He was the moving spirit for the useful work for India in London.

In his presidential address he enunciated the ideal of the Indian patriots as 'establishment of a Federation of free and separate states—the United States of India on fraternal feelings with the self-governing colonies, each with its local autonomy cemented together, under the aegis of Great Britain'. He said:

- "Strive to show yourselves constantly worthy of your cause. Be tolerant towards all. Remember that moral improvement is the only source of real unity and as such of dignity as well as happiness."

TWENTY-FIRST SESSION—1905 AT BANARAS

This session was presided over by Mr. Gopal Krishna Gokhale, one of the ablest statesmen of his time, about whom Gandhiji said, "Sir Pherozeshah had seemed to me like the Himalayas, Lokmanya like the Ocean, but Gokhale was as the Ganges." Lokmanya Tilak described him as, "The diamond of India, the jewel of Maha-rashtra and prince among workers."

GOPAL KRISHNA GOKHALE

Following are some of the extracts from Gokhale's address:

- "It is a sad truth that to the end of his administration Lord Curzon did not really understand the people of India. Lord Curzon denounced in unmeasured terms not only the present generation of Indians, but also their remote ancestors, and even the ideals of their race."

- "The true Swadeshi Movement is both a patriotic and an economic movement. The idea of Swadeshi or of one's own country is one of the noblest conceptions that have ever stirred the heart of humanity."

In this session, there were echoes of division of opinion among Congressmen. Nationalists opposed the resolution of welcome to Prince and Princess of Wales, and when put to vote they walked out.

4

PARTITION OF BENGAL

PARTITION OF BENGAL—1905

In 1903 Lord Curzon decided to partition Bengal into two new Provinces of Bengal and Assam. This was done on the ostensible ground of administrative convenience but with sinister object of augmenting communal bickering between Hindus and Muslims. This transformed the entire scene and the Congress too in the process. Moderates like Bipin Chandra Pal, Lal Mohan Ghosh now became extremists and dominated the political arena along with Aurobindo Ghosh. By 1905–6 the agitation took a violent turn against this decision. Public meetings were held. Hundreds of memorials were submitted and one was sent to the Secretary of the State with more than 70,000 signatures of the people of Eastern Bengal.

Sh. Gopal Krishna Gokhale pleaded with the Viceroy in the Legislative Council, 'My Lord, conciliate Bengal'. He even visited England to convince British Government of the wrong done to Bengal and India.

Boycott of the foreign goods and propagation of Swadeshi became a weapon for political fight.

Whole country was behind Bengal. This agitation, involving protest meetings, continued for two years. Inspite of all this, Bengal's partition was brought into effect on 16th October, 1905. On that day, the country saw popular demonstrations unparalleled in Indian History. Thousands fasted and went barefooted as a mark of mourning. On that day yellow threads were bound round the wrists of Bengalees as a symbol of brotherhood and vow was taken to undo the wicked partition.

'Vande Mataram' became the war cry.

Mr. Morley, Secretary of State for India admitted that partition of Bengal was against the wishes of the people of Bengal, but dismissed its annulment as the same 'is a settled fact.'

Swadeshi movement, boycott of foreign goods, and demand for swaraj spread to the remotest villages. Due to Lord Curzon's unimaginative actions the seeds for self-government and swaraj were sown, which brought a mass awakening, the like India had not witnessed in the past half a century.

This lead to extremist activities in Bengal. Literature of Raja Ram Mohan Roy, Vidya Sagar, Bankim Chandra Chatterjee and forceful writings of Aurobindo Ghosh influenced young Bengalees. Supression was at the peak. Unparalleled sacrifice brought no relief. It gave birth to violent activities and many revolutionary organisations were formed. These included:

1. Calcutta Anusilan Samiti
2. East Club of Calcutta
3. Yugantar Group of Calcutta
4. Saraswati Samiti of Calcutta
5. The Suharid Samiti of Mymensingh
6. The Bandhah Samiti of Barisal
7. The Yuva Samiti of Faridpur
8. Jan Mangal Samiti of Bogra
9. Deccan Anusilan Samiti of Dacca and its branches

The basis of these organisations was loyalty to a particular nationalist individual leaders. Some of the events occurring after 1907 include:

1. At Muzzafarpur attempt was made on the life of Presidency magistrate Mr. Kingford, killing Mrs. and Miss Kennedy, as a result Khudiram Bose was hanged.
2. Approver Naren Goswami was murdered. As a result Kansi Datt and Satyen Bose were hanged.
3. An attempt was made on the life of Lt. Governor. As a result Beepan Bose was convicted and sentenced to life imprisonment.
4. Murders of many police officers took place.

These activities made governance from Calcutta most difficult.

In the year 1911, taking advantage of the coronation of the King Emperor, it was decided to change the Capital of India from Calcutta to Delhi and partition of Bengal was amended in such a way that Bengalee speaking areas were kept intact.

It was clear that significant sections of the Indian public had become weary of the British misrule. They were now impatient to get rid of their subject status and were determined to have self-government. Although the Congress preferred well planned movements, and constitutional struggle, political terrorism was making head way as evident by the emergence of martyrs like Jatin Bagha, Khudiram Bose and their followers. The Congress could not remain unaffected by the political environs. The cleavage between the moderates and the militant wing under Lokmanya Tilak had considerably escalated.

However, the British policies to counter the nationalist movement were also more effectively pursued. The year 1906 also witnessed the birth of All India Muslim League founded at Dacca at the inspiration of the Imperial Government. Mohd. Ali Jinnah, then, was Private Secretary to Dadabhai Naoroji—President of the Indian National Congress. Later on in 1913 he joined the newly formed Muslim League and within next few years occupied its presidential seat. Jinnah continued to masquerade as a nationalist as long as it suited his convenience. Later, when Gandhiji embarked upon the non-cooperation campaign, Jinnah left the Congress in 1920. Jinnah had a peacock ego and now looked upon himself and his Muslim followers as the third and a decisive force. Essentially a moderate, Jinnah was unable to face prospects of courting imprisonment and had no liking for Gandhiji's programme. He preferred communal parties as an alibi to cover his personal inadequacy.

TWENTY-SECOND SESSION—1906 AT CALCUTTA

This session was presided over by Dadabhai Naoroji. At the age of 81, he came all the way from England to preside over this session in order to effect the conciliation between the moderates and more aggressive nationalists.

In his address, he said:

- 'We do not ask for favours, we want only justice. We want Self-government or Swaraj like that of United Kingdom or Dominions.' He further said: 'Freedom is the very breath of our life. We stand for liberty. The whole of the administration in every department must be in the hands of people.'

Main resolution of the session was related to Partition of Bengal, Boycott and Swadeshi. For the first time in the history of Congress, boycott was authorised as a political weapon. Moderate leaders dissented and the resolution on Swaraj was passed which was taken as triumph of Lokmanya Tilak.

TWENTY-THIRD SESSION—1907 AT SURAT

This session was to be held at Nagpur, but due to influence of Lokmanya Bal Gangadhar Tilak, the venue was changed to Surat. In the resolutions published for subjects Committee, there was no mention of Calcutta Session's resolution on Swaraj, Swadeshi and Boycott.

Nationalists led by Lokmanya Tilak wanted, on the other hand, the reiteration of the last years resolution. In the Reception Committee Moderates had majority (in those days members of Reception Committee used to elect President). Moderates wanted Dr. Rash Behari Ghosh as President whereas Nationalists were opposed to him. Lokmanya Tilak offered to withdraw all opposition in case *status quo* was not disturbed. Attitude of the Moderates was exasperating, and Tilak Party decided to offer opposition from the very start.

When the name of Dr. Ghosh as President was proposed by Sir Surendra Nath Banerjee, there were shouts. Meeting was adjourned. President could not read his address. In his address he said,

- "What we demand is that our rulers should introduce reforms. We want in reality and not in mere name to be the sons of the Empire. The ideal for which we are striving is autonomy within the Empire and not absolute independence."

- Gokhale remarked to youths, "You do not realise the enormous reserve power behind the Government. If the Congress were to do anything such as you suggest the Government would have no difficulty in throttling in five minutes." Lokmanya Tilak replied, "Certainly there is a very small party which talks about abolishing the British rule at once and completely. That does not concern us. It is much too far in the future. Unorganised, disarmed and still disunited, we should not have a chance of shaking the British suzerainty. We may leave all sorts of things to a distant time."

This session is, therefore, remembered for its unruly scenes depicting acute differences in the moderates and Tilak's followers. Great confusion prevailed. Shoes and leather were used. A shoe hit Sir Pherozeshah Mehta. President Dr. Ghosh's address also contained certain derogatory and offensive remarks against the group led by Lokmanya. Lokmanya was against split in the interest of the country. He advocated in his paper 'Kesri':

- "Both moderates and aggressive nationalists must remember that persons belonging to both groups are actuated by a sincere desire to promote welfare of the country and that neither is deliberately working to bring about the ruin of their country. Both of them should realise that only in unity there is safety and unity they have to keep inspite of differences of opinion. Neither should try to stamp out the other. The moderates should remember that it is because of the new party (i.e. nationalists have come into the existence) that bureaucracy condescends to rally them."

5

MINTO MORLEY REFORMS—CONGRESS RESISTANCE

TWENTY-FOURTH SESSION—1909 AT LAHORE

MAHAMANA PT. MADAN MOHAN MALVIYA

This session was presided over by Mahamana Pt. Madan Mohan Malviya. The main topic of the session was Minto Morley Reforms and its regulations. These reforms bestowed separate electorate for Mohammedans and some other concessions. Panditji in his address said:

- "Some special concessions such as a Muslim graduate of 5 years is allowed to vote where non-muslim graduates should have 30 years standing, have been given to Mohammedans which have been refused to non-Mohammedans. Let it be remembered that those favours have been shown not out of any love for our Mohammedan brethren but only to keep them quiet, to keep them from standing shoulder to shoulder with their Hindu brothers, to agitate for reforms. This policy of partiality will not live as it does not deserve to live."

Among the resolutions, one was the disapproval of Indian Council Act, 1909 which created separate electorate. This session was remarkable also for another reason. The grievances of Indians in Transval had created profound impression and presence of Mr. H.R. Polak an associate of Gandhiji in South Africa, had brought the question once more to the front.

TWENTY-FIFTH SESSION—1910 AT ALLAHABAD

This session was presided over by Sir William Wedderburn, who presided over the Congress Session once before in 1889. For his abounding love for India and Indians, Gokhale said of him:

- "He believed in us inspite of obloquy of his own countrymen. He has believed in us that he has been able to work through sunshine and storm and through good report and evil report. The picture of this great venerable Rishi of modern times, who has done this work for us, is a picture that is too venerable, too beautiful and too inspiring for words. It is a picture to contemplate in silence."

Sir William Wedderburn was specially requested to preside over the session to cement the bonds of unity between Hindus and Muslims. In his speech he said:

- "I have passed a quarter of a century among you and in one respect in which I shall not be found wanting, is my goodwill, towards you and the cause you represent. Let us march with our face to the light, put in the sickle and reap. Our watchword must be hope, conciliation and united efforts." He further said, "A good illustration what may be achieved by the Hindus and Mohammedans standing together in the service of India, is supplied by the latest news from South Africa where Hindus and Musalmans unitedly fought for their rights under the leadership of Mahatma Gandhi."

Among the resolutions adopted were, opposition to separate electorate and its extension to local bodies, Press Act, Seditious Meetings Act and annually increasing Military expenses.

This year of 1911 was marked by one of the greatest changes in the administration to commemorate the visit of King by transfer of capital from Calcutta to Delhi and annulment of the partition of Bengal.

TWENTY-SIXTH SESSION—1911 AT CALCUTTA

It was hoped that Mr. Ramsay Macdonald of the Labour Party of England (who became Prime Minister of England in twenties) who was in India at that time would preside, but the death of Mrs. Macdonald called him away from India and Pandit Bishan Narain Dar was unexpectedly asked to preside over this session. Pt. Bishan Narain Dar was one of the most learned and yet modest man of United Provinces. Some of the extracts from his address are:

- "The greatest wound in the heart of India was the partition of Bengal, the most unwise and unfortunate measure of a reactionary Viceroy. The annulment of the same is the triumph of the constitutional agitation.
- Delhi is the eternal city of Hindustan and is associated with the most glorious and romantic memories of both Hindus and Mohammedans and this change of the capital of India from Calcutta to Delhi will be most deeply appreciated by Indians.
- The root cause of most of our misfortunes, which if not corrected, forebodes serious disorders in the future, is the growth of unsympathetic and illiberal spirit in the bureaucracy towards new born hopes and ideals of Indian people."

Resolution regarding abolition of indenture labour in South Africa and congratulation to Gandhiji upon the repeal of Anti-Asiatic legislation of South Africa were adopted.

TWENTY-SEVENTH SESSION—1912 AT BANKIPUR

This session was presided over by Mr. R.N. Mudholkar—a laborious student of Indian politics covering a wide range of interests including agricultural indebtedness, poverty and economic uplift, technical education etc. In his address he said:

- "The sons of India have before them a high and mighty task, which is as noble as arduous. The inheritors of great civilization, lofty ideals and stirring traditions, the people of this great land, have glorious mission to create a nation by the fusion of various races, creeds and castes, and to weld together communities which have been in sharp antagonism to each other. The people of India have a great mission to fulfill, a great part to play in the progress of the world and it is to enable us to effectually perform this sacred duty that we are striving to reach our goal."

This session was overshadowed by an attempted outrage on the life of Lord Hardinge.

TWENTY-EIGHTH SESSION—1913 AT KARACHI

This session was presided over by Nawab Syed Mohammed. Some of the extracts of his address are:

- "The Congress has, from its very inception, set before itself the ideal of a united Indian nationality, and has been consistently advocating the cause of the Indian people as a whole, without being influenced by party or sectarian considerations, incompatible with that high ideal. The Congress well deserves the credit for the immense changes brought about in the Government of the country."

He appreciated the resolution of All India Muslim League which had adopted a resolution stating that the future development of the country depended on the harmonious working and cooperation of various communities.

This session saw the beginning of Hindu-Muslim unity. This session expressed satisfaction at the recognition of the Govt. of India of the necessity of Provincial Autonomy.

TWENTY-NINTH SESSION—1914 AT MADRAS

This session was presided over by Sh. Bhupendra Nath Basu—an eminent solicitor, a great orator from Calcutta.

Some of the extracts from his address are:

- "If English rule in India meant the canonisation of a bureaucracy, if it meant perpetual domination and tutelage, it would be a curse to civilisation, and a blot on humanity.

- We are involved in a struggle for life and death. The mind is absorbed in the great issue now hanging in the battle-fields of Europe, where our brethren, British and Indians are mingling their blood in the cause of Honour, Liberty and Justice."

This session demanded higher ranks in the Military be opened for the Indians.

THIRTIETH SESSION—1915 AT BOMBAY

This session was presided over by Sir Satyendra Prasad Sinha who was the first Indian member of the Viceroy's Executive Council. He was the only Indian ever appointed as Under Secretary of the State of India. Also only one Indian to be raised to the peerage (Member of the House of Lords—Second House of the British Parliament). This session was essentially of moderate Congress, speech of the President was very reactionary. This session was the great revival in public interest in the Congress, after Surat Session. The session was attended by 2259 delegates.

Some of the extracts from presidential address are:

- "We want to make it perfectly clear, if we have not done so already that there is no one among us willing to cause the slightest embarrassment to the Government. We seek no capital out of the service so ungrudgingly rendered by our countrymen to the Empire. There is not, I trust, a single person in our camp who expects reforms, as the price or the reward of our loyalty."
- "Day will not break the sooner because we get up before twilight."

Usual resolutions for more powers and loyalty towards Government were adopted.

THIRTY-FIRST SESSION—1916 AT LUCKNOW

This session was presided over by Hon'ble Ambika Charan Mozumdar—a prominent lawyer, associated with Congress since its birth—author of famous book entitled 'Indian National Revolution'.

Some of the extracts of his presidential address are:

- "If the United Congress were buried at Surat it is reborn today at Lucknow, in the garden of Wajid Ali Shah."
- "Lord Morley once said that he cannot give us the moon but we were never so moonstruck as to ask for the moon and his Lordship has no fears that he has given us more substantial than mere moonshine."
- "In a despotic form of Government everything is done for the people and nothing by the people. Its greatest drawback is that it makes the people, whom it governs, impotent to help themselves.
- "Indian Press with all its difficulties and disabilities has played an important part in the evolution of National life.
- "Slaves at home can never be treated as freemen abroad. Be ambitious, but not proud, be humble, but aspire to a nobler, manlier and healthier life."
- "Firm and resolute in your purpose, be always manly and dignified in your attitude, and sober and cautious in your hopes. There is no royal road to freedom.

  What avail your wealth, your learning,
  Empty titles sordid trade.
  True Self-rule were worth them all,
  Nations by themselves are made."

The session was historic in many respects. Mrs. Annie Besant, candidate of Nationalists got 25 votes and Mr. Mozumdar got 62 votes. Instead of this defeat of the Nationalists at the hand of Moderates, they decided to participate. This session was attended by Bipin Chandra Pal, Tilak, Besant among other Nationalists.

Resolution in support of Swadeshi movement was adopted.

THIRTY-SECOND SESSION—1917 AT CALCUTTA

This session was presided over by Annie Besant—an Irish woman—who made India as her home, a matchless orator, soul of worldwide Theosophical Society of India, who started

Home Rule Movement. She was interned in the middle of 1917 with Messrs Arundale and Wadia.

ANNIE BESANT

Some of the extracts from her address are:

- "For the first time in Congress history you have chosen as your president one who, when your choice was made, was under the heavy ban of Government displeasure and who lay interned as a person dangerous to public safety. While I was humiliated, you crowned me with honour, while I was crushed under the heels of bureaucratic power, you acclaimed me as your leader. While I was silenced and unable to defend myself, you defended and won for me my release. I was proud to serve in the lowliest fashion as a soldier but you have lifted me and placed me before the world as your chosen representative. My deeds must speak for me. My words are too poor."

- "At last India sprang to her feet and cried in the words of one of her noblest sons, 'Freedom is my birth right and I shall have it."

  She quoted the words of Swami Vivekanand,

- "Our ancestors are great, we must recall that. We must learn the element of our being, the blood that courses in our veins, we must have faith in that blood, and build an India, yet greater than She was before."

- "Self-government is necessary to the self-respect and dignity of a people."

This year Sir Montague Secretary of State for India visited India.

Congress expressed its grateful satisfaction over the pronouncement of the Imperial Government that its object was the establishment of responsible Government in India.

Events moved fast in the year 1918. The long expected Montague Chelmsford report was released on 12 July, 1918, introducing dyarchy in the administration. This report created a rift among the Nationalist leaders in the Congress. Shortly after a Conference of right wing of the Congress under the chairmanship of Sir Surendra Nath Banerjee, was held at Calcutta and welcomed the Reforms Scheme. But on 14th July, 1918, these proposals were condemned in Bengal Provincial Conference. Special session of the Congress was called at Bombay under the presidentship of Syed Hasan Imam. Most of the Moderates and right wing leaders did not attend. This session declared that the people of India are fit for responsible Government and repudiates the assumption to the contrary contained in the report on Indian Constitutional Reforms.

In April, 1918, Gandhiji attended a meeting of the Indian leaders called by the Viceroy Lord Chelmsford to devise a scheme for overcoming shortage of recruits.

THIRTY-THIRD SESSION—1918 AT DELHI

This session was presided over by Pandit Madan Mohan Malviya (Lokmanya Tilak was to preside but could not come in time from England). Panditji in his address said:

- "Standing in this ancient capital of India both of the Hindu and Mohammedan periods, it fills me, my countrymen with inexpressible sorrow and shame to think that we the descendants of Hindus who ruled for 4,000 years over this extensive empire and the descendants of Musalmans who ruled here for several hundred years should have so far fallen from our ancient state that we should have to argue our capacity for even a limited measure of autonomy and self-rule."

This session was a marked success. For the first time more than 1000 peasants attended the session.

It was resolved that the recommendations of Rowlatt Committee if given effect to would interfere with fundamental right of the Indian people.

It was also demanded that in view of the President Wilson (USA) and Mr. Lloyd George (Britain) and other statesmen that to ensure the future peace of the World, the principle of self-determination should be applied to all progressive nations including India.

Shri K. Subramaniam, K.C.I.E., Doctor of Laws, retired Judge of Madras High Court, President of Home Rule League in India addressed a long letter in 1917 to President Wilson, in which he stated, 'Honoured Sir, the aching heart of India cries out to you, whom we believe to be an instrument of God in the reconstruction of the World.'

Viceroy conveyed his displeasure in most undignified language to Shri K. Subramaniam. Questions in this regard were also put in the House of Commons. Mr. Montague replied:

> 'The impropriety of this disgraceful letter is all the more inexcusable owing to the position of the writer. The assertions in the letter are too wild and baseless to require or receive notice from any responsible authority.'

Shri Subramaniam renounced the title of K.C.I.E. and returned the insignia as a protest against unbecoming and undignified language used by Secretary of State for India.

6

SATYAGRAHA AGAINST THE ROWLATT ACT—1919

Meritorious and ungrudging services were rendered by the Indians in World War I (1914–18), which were highly appreciated by the Viceroy—Secretary of State. British Press and public paid tributes for these services. When the honour of Britain was at stake, the apostle of non-violence Mahatma Gandhi even attended a conference of the Indian leaders called by the Viceroy in 1918 to find out ways and means to fill the shortage of army recruits. Gandhiji went from village to village to enrol recruits. After victory, when India expected the right of self-determination or a Government of its own choice, Rowlatt Act was presented to India as a reward for its distinguished collaboration during the war. This Act invested Government with powers to arrest and detain anyone without assigning reasons. All rights, enjoyed so far, were scrapped and there was "No Vakil, No Dalil, No Appeal" (no pleader, no argument, no appeal). This Act was vehemently opposed by public and the members of Imperial Council. Mr. Sriniwas Shastri made a very reasoned and forceful speech in the Council for the withdrawal of the bill, but no heed was paid.

Gandhiji came to the front. He said:

> "A Government be it ever so powerful and autocratic, is bound to yield to unanimous public opinion. It is bad luck for us, if truth and justice have to surrender to mere physical force whether it is wielded by an individual or a government."
>
> "The Rowlatt Bills were the unmistakable symptoms of the deep seated disease in the Governing body", Gandhi asserted.

Gandhiji announced on 24th February, 1919 that he would lead a 'Passive Resistance Satyagraha' if the Rowlatt Bills were passed. On 1st March he appealed to Indians to pledge that in the event of these bills becoming law, they would refuse to obey these laws. There was a good response from all parts of India to Gandhi's appeal. Countrywide Hartal was called for 30th March which was later changed to 6th April. In Delhi it was observed on 30th March as all arrangements had already been made. A huge procession led by Swami Shradhanand was taken out. Some European soldiers threatened firing. Swamiji bared his chest and invited the soldiers to shoot him. It infused a new spirit. At Delhi Railway Station, there were some disturbances resulting in 5 deaths and injuries to scores.

On 6th April, Hartal was observed throughout India—every town and even villages. Our countrymen's total identification with the movement of freedom and the concept of Gandhian Satyagraha cannot be better expressed than what Gandhi himself described in his autobiography—"My Experiments With Truth". He graphically recalled therein the basic constituents and the tenor of the said movement in the following words:

> "I had hardly begun to feel my way towards recovery when I happened casually to read in the papers the Rowlatt Committee's report which had just been published. Its recommendations startled me. Shankerlal Banker and Umar Sobhani approached me with the suggestion that I should take some prompt action in this matter. In about a month I went to Ahmedabad. I mentioned my apprehensions to Vallabhbhai who used to come to see me almost daily. 'Something must be done,' said I to him. 'But what can we do in the circumstances ?' he asked. In reply, I answered: 'If even a handful of men can be found to sign the pledge of resistance, if the proposed measure is passed into law, in defiance of it, we ought to offer Satyagraha at once. If I were not laid up like this I should give battle against it all alone and expect others to follow suit. But in my present helpless condition I feel myself to be altogether unequal to the task.' As a result of this talk

it was decided to call a small meeting of such persons as were in touch with me. The recommendations of the Rowlatt Committee seemed to be altogether unwarranted by the evidence published in the report, and were, I feel, such that no self-respecting people could submit to them. The proposed conference was at last held at the Ashram. So far as I remember among those who attended were Vallabhbhai, Shrimati Sarojini Naidu, Sjt Shankerlal Banker and Shrimati Anusuya Ben. The Satyagraha pledge was drafted at this meeting and as far as I can recollect, was signed by all present. A separate body called the Satyagraha Sabha, was established at my instance. I became the President of the Sabha. It seemed clear to me that the Sabha was not likely to live long. I could see that already my emphasis on Truth and Ahimsa had begun to be disliked by some of its members. Nevertheless in its early stages our new activity went on at full blast, and the movement gathered momentum rapidly and the Government grew more and more determined to give effect to its recommendations, and the Rowlatt Bill was published. Shastriji delivered an impassioned speech in the Imperial Legislative Council in which he uttered a solemn note of warning to the Government. The Viceroy seemed to be listening spell-bound riveted on Shastriji as the latter poured forth the hot stream of his eloquence. For the moment it seemed to me as if the Viceroy could not but be deeply moved by it. It was so true and full of feeling, but this warning was entirely lost upon the Government.

"I earnestly pleaded with the Viceroy. I clearly told him that the Government's action left me no other course except to resort to Satyagraha. But it was all in vain. I felt myself at a loss to discover how to offer Civil Disobedience against the Rowlatt Bill if it was finally passed into law. The Rowlatt Bill had been published as an Act. I was in the twilight condition between sleep and consciousness, when suddenly the idea broke upon me. I was as if in a dream which was:

"We should call upon the country to observe a general Hartal. Satyagraha is a process of self-purification and ours is a sacred fight, and it seems to me to be in the fitness of things that it should be commenced with an act of self-purification. Let all the people of India therefore suspend their business on that day, and observe the day as one of fasting, and prayer. I drafted a brief appeal. The date of Hartal was fixed on 30th March, 1919, but was subsequently changed to 6th April.

"The whole of India from one end to the other, towns as well as villages, observed a complete Hartal on that day. It was a most wonderful spectacle. Delhi had observed Hartal on the 30th March. The word of Swami Shradhanand and Hakim Ajmal Khan Sahib was law, and Hindus and Mussalmans seemed united like one. Swami Shradhanandji was invited to deliver a speech in the Juma Masjid which he did. All this was more than authorities could bear. The police opened fire there, causing a number of casualties and the reign of repression commenced in Delhi. Swami Shradhanand urgently summoned me to Delhi. I wired back, saying I would start for Delhi immediately after the 6th of April celebrations were over in Bombay. From Amritsar Dr. Satyapal and Dr. Kitchlew had sent me a pressing invitation to visit Amritsar after Delhi. The Hartal in Bombay was a complete success. Full preparations had been made for starting Civil Disobedience. I suggested people might prepare salt from sea water in disregard of salt laws, or print and sell proscribed literature. This was the easiest way of offering Civil Disobedience. Two of my books were proscribed. A sufficient number of them were therefore printed and it was arranged to sell them at the end of the monster meeting to be held that evening. All the copies were soon sold out. The Government did not think this act to constitute an offence under the law. The news caused general disappointment. The next morning another meeting was held for the administration of the pledges with regard to Swadeshi and Hindu-Muslim unity. Only a handful of persons came. I have noticed the characteristic difference in the popular attitude, partiality for exciting work and dislike for quiet constructive efforts. On the night of 7th April, I started for Delhi and Amritsar. On reaching Muttra on the 8th, I heard rumours about my probable arrest. Before the train had reached Palwal station I was served with a written order to the effect that I was prohibited from entering the boundary of Punjab, as my presence there was likely to result in a disturbance of peace. I was asked by the police to get down from the train. I refused to do so, saying I wanted to go to the Punjab in response to a pressing invitation, not to foment unrest but to allay it. I am therefore sorry that it is not possible for me to comply with the order.

"At Palwal I was taken out of the train, and put under police custody. Inspector Bowring requested me to return to Bombay of my own accord and not to cross the frontier of the Punjab. I replied that I could not possibly comply with the order, and that I was not prepared of my own accord to go back. When we had reached Bombay the police officer-in-charge told me: 'You are now free.' A friend told me that the news of my arrest had incensed the people, and roused them to a pitch of new frenzy. An outbreak was apprehended every minute near Pydhuni. The magistrate and the police had already arrived there. I went to the place. On seeing me the people went mad with joy. A procession was started. We sighted a body of mounted police. The procession found itself confronted by the police, who had arrived there to prevent it from proceeding further in the direction of the Fort. The ranks of the people were soon broken, some got trampled under foot, others were badly mauled and crushed. The whole thing presented a most dreadful spectacle. The horsemen and the people were mixed together in mad confusion.

"I proceeded to Ahmedabad where the mill hands had gone mad over the rumoured arrest of Shrimati Anusuya Ben. They had struck work and committed acts of violence, and a sergeant had been done to death, and an attempt had been made to pull up the rails. The people were terror-stricken. I declared a penitential fast of three days for myself. I made up my mind to suspend Satyagraha so long as people had not learned the lesson of peace. I was firmly of opinion that those who wanted to lead the people to Satyagraha ought to be able to keep the people within the limited non-violence expected of them.

"I had called on the people to launch upon Civil Disobedience before they had thus qualified themselves for it, and this mistake seemed to me of Himalayan magnitude. I realise that before a people could be fit for offering Civil Disobedience they should thoroughly understand its deep implications. That being so, before re-starting Civil Disobedience on a mass scale, it would be necessary to create a band of well-tried, pure-hearted, volunteers who thoroughly understood the strict conditions of Satyagraha. They could explain that to the people and by sleepless vigilance keep them on the right path."

7

JALLIANWALA MASSACRE—13TH APRIL, 1919

Gandhiji was arrested on way to Delhi. This led to widespread agitation in the principal cities and in the countryside, particularly in Gujarat involving the city of Ahmedabad. In the Punjab, Lahore, Kasur, Gujranwala and several other places witnessed oppression, raping and arson at the hands of British police. In Punjab too, people were no less agitated. During the First World War trade in hide and skins was badly hit, as the Germans were the principal buyers. Prices had risen rocket high. There was general unrest due to continued oppressive measures by the British administration even after the war. The Rowlatt Act, which deprived people of their basic human rights broke the camel's back. Though the Government belatedly explained provisions of this Act by way of propaganda, handbills, various rumors spread and the people at large felt that their family life was being threatened by an oppressive regime. Hindus, Muslims and the Sikhs all were united against the Raj, as they got only the Rowlatt Act, while they were expecting a generous doze of constitutional reforms as a gesture of goodwill for India's massive contribution to the war effort. They were completely disillusioned. Gandhiji showed them a new and effective way of resistance.

Now, the crown of glory was reserved for Amritsar, the holy city of the Sikhs, which saw the historic ghastly massacre by British forces. The Lt. Governor apprehended a large scale revolt comparable to the Mutiny of 1857. The then Lt. Governor Sir Michael O'Dwyer was a hard liner imperialist. He was hell bent on teaching Indians a lesson. The Army

Chief in Punjab, Brigadier-General Dyer was no less contemptuous of the Indians.

On March 30, 1919, there was a successful strike (Hartal) by all sections of people throughout Punjab. The Provincial Government detained popular leaders like Dr. Satya Pal and Dr. Saifuddin Kitchlew, a veteran barrister and they became the symbols of Hindu-Muslim unity. These eminent leaders always discouraged violence and yet they were put behind the bars, which greatly infuriated the people. One Hansraj, a British agent, who had accompanied these detained leaders upto Deputy Commissioner's office spread all kinds of wild rumors to further inflame the situation, thus, to provide a handle to Michael O'Dwyer to put his machinery of oppression to work his vendetta against the Indians.

The people, because of wild rumors, felt infuriated. They were now leaderless and went on a rampage. Even some friendly British officials, including a kindly medical doctor, Miss Sherwood, was killed in the fray. The Deputy Commissioner Sir Miles Irving lost his nerve and urgently called in the military forces to intervene. The Lt. Governor readily agreed to his request. Martial law was proclaimed all over the Punjab and Brigadier-General Dyer was handed over charge of the district. Dyer was a sick man and because of an accident was a psychiatric case. He clamped down curfew, but a large number of people, unaware of his orders, came from surrounding areas to celebrate "Baisakhi", the festival of the spring. As was customary, men, women and children in thousands flocked in the Jallianwala Bagh (in Amritsar city) to participate in the celebrations.

Meanwhile Hansraj, the British agent-provacateur, arranged a public meeting in the Bagh to protest against arrest of the leaders. The people gathered at the meeting without realising implications of the ban on the meeting.

General Dyer, who was predetermined to wreck vengeance on the Indians, surrounded the Jallianwala Bagh—the venue of meeting—with his soldiers, who were all mercenary Indians and Gorkha soldiers. Without giving any warning to the assembled people, Dyer asked his men to fire on the unarmed crowd. The Bagh had enclosing walls on three sides and there was only a small exit. Some 20,000 men had gathered at this meeting. About sixteen hundred rounds were fired, killing about 500 people, injuring and mutilating hundreds.

The story of this frightful experience, which gave Punjab the crowning glory of the martyrdom in the struggle for freedom, is well documented in subsequent official and non-official enquiries. The British Cabinet papers, which were previously not available, under the Fifty Year Rule, are now open to scholars and these testify to the rectitude of anger of Indian jurists—Motilal Nehru and others who had, through an un-official inquiry, laid bare the responsibility for this dastardly massacre of Dyer under inspiration of his chief, the notorious Michael O'Dwyer.

Dyer was not satisfied even with this ghastly and cowardly massacre. To revenge the outrage against Miss Sherwood, Dyer issued an order which required that no Indian must be allowed to walk on the roads in the neighbourhood of Sherwood's murder site at Amritsar and if he did go through, he must do so on all fours. This was interpreted as "crawling order". All people who lived in the street or had to pass through were made to crawl after the manners of worms and reptiles. Even a blind man had to do the same. The old and young, rich and poor, the thin and fat, all had to submit this atrocious order. If by any chance crawling was not satisfactorily done by a person, he was struck down to the ground with the rifle butts of the British soldiers, whose behaviour was generally offensive. In those days, it had become extremely so, and men and women were made to crawl again and again. It is difficult to imagine the sufferings and hardships of the residents of that lane. The scavengers did not go to their houses which were rendered extremely dirty and filthy. Summary courts were set up under the Martial Law, the press was gagged, movements restricted. More serious cases were tried at Lahore by a Law Commission, which awarded punishments on adhoc basis. Flogging was the most common punishment. In Lahore 80 persons were flogged, in Kasur 85 and in Amritsar 38. For waging war against the King Emperor, 581 were convicted, 108 were sentenced to death, 264 to transportation for life. Even a boy of 11 and a man of over 100 were not spared. The Reviewing Commission did not agree that such oppression was at all unjustifiable, nor that the allegation of waging war against the King Emperor was at all true. Finally, the Indian National Congress appointed an Enquiry Committee under Pt. Madan Mohan Malviya, who was respected for his probity and integrity by the Indians and the British alike.

Jawaharlal Nehru, who had by now risen to the status of a popular and competent young leader, rushed to Jallianwala Bagh for gathering material for the Congress Committee Report. By sheer chance, on a train journey he happened to be in the same compartment in which Brig. General Dyer was travelling. He heard Dyer, speaking to his fellow officer, boasting, that he felt "like reducing the rebellion city (of Amritsar) to a heap of ashes."

The British Government appointed Lord Hunter to go into the related matters. Divided counsels prevailed in the Hunter Committee where European members of the Committee and the Indian members clashed on various issues. Even, the majority report signed by the European members of the Committee censured Dyer for firing without warning. It did not accept the view that there was a conspiracy to overthrow the government. The Secretary of State, Mr. Montague, was inclined to accept the minority report of Indian members of the Committee, which was similar to Congress Committee Report. But Montague was thwarted by the Viceroy and British bureaucrats. Dyer, however, was compulsorily retired from the Indian army and deported to England.

Dr. M.R. Jayakar offered the following testimony with regard to the Enquiry Committee appointed by the Congress:

"The report is an admirable production for the care and restraint with which the facts have been stated and conclusion arrived at." When Jayakar showed this report to a fellow European lawyer, Mr. Inverarity, and disclosed to him that it was drafted by Mahatma Gandhi. Inverarity commented that the report "would have much damaging effect in Britain than in India." In England, however, in the Commons, Montague, contrary to his previously expressed views, supported the beastly action of Dyer stating that he was right in firing upon the gathering at Jallianwala. The condemnation of Dyer came from an unexpected quarter, when Mr. Winston

Churchill emphatically stated that Dyer was not unjustly punished but deserved disciplinary action. Churchill said:

> "One tremendous fact stands out, I mean, the slaughter of nearly four hundred persons and the wounding of probably three to four times that number at the Jallianwala Bagh on 13th April. This is an episode which appears to me to be without those tragic occurrences which take place when troops are brought into collision with the civic population. It is an extraordinary event, a monstrous event which stands in singular and sinister isolation..."

Lord Curzon in the House of Lords was shocked and expressed the opinion that Dyer had not saved India. But the Lords, which had a preponderance of Imperial aristocrats voted for Dyer's action. But the deed had shocked the perpetrators even. The London 'Times' commented "passion had over-ridden reason" and the vote has gone against the weight of argument.

Yet, imperialist sections hailed Dyer as saviour of the Empire. A British Newspaper, "The Morning Post" raised funds in his defence. The amount raised was considerable. The Imperial poet Laureate Rudyard Kipling donated Pounds 10 to this fund. The Statesman, Calcutta remitted Rs. 20,000 and contributions were also offered to Dyer's Defence Fund by "Madras Mail" and "Civil & Military Gazette" Lahore. Sir Sankaran Nair, a former member of the Viceroy's Executive Council was also critical of Michael O'Dwyer's support to Dyer. He had to pay damages for this criticism in a libel suite brought against him by Sir Michael.

Dyer, who was supported by Michael O'Dwyer, the Lt. Governor, declared before the Hunter Committee:

> "My mind was made up as soon as I came along in my motor car. I had made up my mind that I would do all the men to death. I considered it a duty. I wanted to teach them a lesson so that they might not laugh at me. I would have fired and fired longer, if I had required ammunition. I had taken an armoured car but found that the passage to the Bagh could not admit it and so I left it behind. I thought I should shoot well and shoot strong so that I or anybody else should not have to shoot again."

Rattan Devi, whose husband was killed in this genocide, lamented:

> "It is impossible for me to describe what I felt. Heaps of dead bodies lay there, some on their backs and some with their faces unturned. A number of them were innocent poor children. I was all along the whole night in the solitary jungle. Nothing but the barking of dogs, or the braying of donkeys was audible. Amidst hundreds of corpses, I passed my night crying and walking."

For India, it was a turning point, for England it was the end of the Empire, as the emotional bonds with their subject dominion—was broken and broken beyond redemption.

India's poet Laureate, Rabindra Nath Tagore speaking of the ghastly deeds of Dyer and O'Dwyer which eventually were known to all had said that truth had "trickled through gagged silence." He renounced the Knighthood bestowed upon him by the British Sovereign. Imperial Britain made light of this massacre and compounded its guilt by following it up with the introduction in the Parliament of the Reforms Bill based on the unpopular "Montford" proposals. This added salt to the injury.

According to Shakespeare, "MURDER MUST OUT". It did with a vengeance. Two decades after this monstrous massacre of Jallianwalla, a heroic son of India, Udham Singh shot dead Sir Michael O'Dwyer, the notorious Lt. Governor, responsible for this misdeed, and the Secretary of State Lord Zetland. This happened on 13th March, 1940, when both Sir Michael O'Dwyer and Lord Zetland were in attendance in a seminar on Afghanistan organised by the Royal Central Asian Society and the East Indian Association in Caxton Hall, London. After the shooting fray, Udham Singh could have easily escaped. He stood there like a gallant knight, who have avenged the tragic massacre of his countrymen at Jallianwala Bagh. He proclaimed that he had killed the enemies of his country. He was produced before a London Court on April 2, 1940, which awarded death sentence on Udham Singh. He was hanged in Pentovill Prison, London on 3rd July, 1940. Udham Singh justified his act of revenge saying that he killed Michael O'Dwyer as he had a grudge against him. Singh added:

- "O'Dwyer was the real culprit. He wanted to crush the spirit of my people. So, I have crushed him. For full twenty one years, I have been trying to wreck vengeance. I am happy I have done the job."
- "I am not scared of death. I want to die young. What is the use of dying when you get old and useless. I am dying for my people. I am dying for my country."

He was happy on shooting the Secretary of State, Lord Zetland too, on similar political grounds. Political terrorism is bad. But those who kill by sword, perish by sword. Udham Singh is considered a martyr in the cause of freedom. But for the Jallianwala massacre, perhaps he would have been a good craftsman, which he actually had been in his early age.

The massacre at Jallianwala had been a turning point in history. The Indian people had lost all faith in the British Empire. The Congress Party also became more aggressive. Its future campaigns were massive movements for the dethronement of the Raj.

THIRTY-FOURTH SESSION—1919 AT AMRITSAR

This session was presided over by Pt. Motilal Nehru. Only a year before he had held back Jawaharlal Nehru from joining the Satyagraha Sabha started by Gandhiji. But, now, after the Jallianwala tragedy, Motilal Nehru was completely transformed into a desperate revolutionary warrior for freedom. He even gave up legal practice and joined Gandhiji following his son in the great battle for freedom.

PT. MOTILAL NEHRU

This session was unique one in view of Jallianwala Bagh massacre, and law Regime, tyrannies and tortures, sorrows and sufferings, depression and repression, agony and anguish, misery and affliction, grief and sadness were written on the walls of Amritsar, on every face, on every particle of dust of that sacred city. Session under these conditions seemed impossible, but due to Swami Shardhanand (Chairman) and Lala Girdhari Lal (Secretary of the Reception Committee), it could be possible. All important leaders such as Pt. Madan Mohan Malviya, Mahatma Gandhi, Lokmanya Tilak, Maulana Shaukat Ali, Maulana Mohammed Ali attended the session.

Some of the extracts from the Presidential address are:

- "What is our ultimate goal ? We want freedom of thought, freedom of action, freedom to fashion our own destiny and build up an India suited to the genius of her people."
- "We must aim at an India where all are free and have fullest opportunities of development, where women have ceased to be in bondage, and the rigours of caste system have disappeared, where there are no privileged classes, or communities, where education is free and open to all, where the capitalist and the landlord do not oppress the labourer and the ryot, where labour is respected and is well paid, and the poverty the curse of the present generation is a thing of the past."

Resolution regarding reforms, condemnation of the excesses and recall of Lord Chelmsford were adopted. Resolution regarding recall of Lord Chelmsford was opposed by one Mr. B.N. Sharma, who was rewarded handsomely by being appointed as a member of the Viceroy's Executive Council.

8

TILAK'S DEATH—END OF AN EPOCH

LOKMANYA BAL GANGADHAR TILAK

Lokmanya Bal Gangadhar Tilak, the most outstanding personality of the pre-Gandhian era passed away on 1st August, 1920. When Gandhiji was ready to begin his non-violent campaign against the 'Raj', Tilak was lying ill in 'Sardar Grih', Bombay. His condition had become so critical that a day before, a Hindi Daily "Bhavishya" published from Allahabad carried Sunder Lal's emotional editorial mourning Tilak's death. Such anticipatory obituary has possibly resulted from Sunder Lal's journalistic sixth sense.

Tilak's colleague Aurobindo Ghosh, who with Bipin Chandra Pal, had been most active in the "Vande Mataram" agitation, resulting from the partition of Bengal had already retired from politics some years ago. He opted to settle in Pondicherry to follow spiritual pursuits. But Tilak remained active in the Congress as an inveterate enemy of the British imperialism. He was foremost in declaring that "Swaraj", or self-government was the goal of his country. This was his birth right and he "must have it." His vigorous role before and after the Bengal partition followed by his incarceration in a British prison in Burma, participation in the Home Rule Movement, his historic defence in Law courts. Also in the

Valentine Chirol defamation case but above all his deep patriotic interest in the Revolutionary Movement in compassing the freedom of India place him among the most conscientious and authentic creators of the freedom movement.

Tilak had become an eye sore in the eyes of the British even before the Congress came in existence. He had helped to found seditious journals as the "Kesri" and the "Mahratta" in January, 1881. In these journals, he made critical remarks about the "Raj" and against the pro-British Dewans of some princely states. For instance, he alleged that Raja T. Madhav Rao, the Dewan of Baroda State exercised control on the Gaikwar, Maharaja Sanjay Rao III, when he did not allow to read even the quarterly journal of Poona Sarvajanik Sabha. Tilak and Gopal Ganesh Agarkar had published letters in the "Kesri" and the "Mahratta" exposing a diabolic conspiracy on the part of Dewan Barve and the British Resident who had planned to physically liquidate the young Maharaja of Kolhapur. Tilak and Agarkar were prosecuted and suffered prison terms for defamation of the Dewan. However, it transpired that the said Maharaja of Kolhapur, while in British prison in Ahmed Nagar Fort, was actually flogged to death on the Christmas Day, 1883. When the dying Maharaja asked for Ganges water in his last moments, whisky was poured down his throat. This episode established the validity of Tilak's suspicion expressed two years earlier and led to widespread resentment in Western India.

Again, virtually at a time when the Congress was inaugurated, Tilak had a row with the Imperial Governor of Bombay, Lord Reay. His lordship had suggested to the Deccan Education Society that they ought to employ European professors if they wanted to take over the Deccan College. Tilak objected vehemently to this racist direction.

As a scholar, too, Tilak owned abilities of the highest order. His literary works showed a well informed magnified mind. His best quoted book, "Geeta Rahasya", which he wrote in Burma jail gave a new interpretation to Lord Krishna's sermon to Arjun on the field of battle of the "Mahabharata". This became a "Bible of Action" for freedom fighters and continues, after having been translated in many Indian and foreign languages, to inspire even today all types of people—

scholars, politicians, soldiers and others. He was the doyen of India's nationalist leadership.

The great Lenin, founder of the Bolshevik State of the U.S.S.R. had paid frequent tributes to Tilak. Lenin referring to Tilak's imprisonment had observed that "the infamous sentence pronounced by the British jackals against the Indian democrat Tilak—(Tilak was sentenced to a long term of exile. A question in the British House of Commons the other day revealed that the Indian jurors had insisted on acquittal and that the verdict had been passed by the Vote of British Jurors!)—this reprisal against a democrat by the lackeys of the money-bags evoked street demonstrations and strike in Bombay."[1]

After the Surat Session, Tilak did not allow himself or his followers to 'get absorbed in controversy regarding the break-up of the Congress'. He discussed in a series of articles the subject of conducting meetings conferences and Congress sessions, duties, functions and privileges of the President and on other constitutional, topical and fundamental subjects. His articles were cogent, thought-provoking and showed his patriotism and intellectual integrity. He was convinced that the driving force in the Congress and in the country must be militant patriots, but the clash against the Moderates was not desirable. Several times he was jailed for sedation.

After Muzaffarpur bomb outrage, the British Government lost its nerves and decided to put Tilak behind the bars. Cases of sedation were fabricated against him on sketchy evidence forged by the prosecutors. He was arrested on June 24, 1908. One of the allegations against him was stated to be the breach of Section 124 A of the CPC for an article that appeared in his paper "Kesri", dated June 9, 1908. The trial opened on 13th July, 1908. Tilak argued his case with conspicuous ability. His defence speech lasted for 21 hours before Justice Davar. At the initiative of the Crown, a special jury was impanelled to try Tilak. Addressing them, Tilak said:

- "I am now on the wrong side of life and for me, it can only be a matter for few years, but future generation would

---

[1] Lenin—*The National Liberation Movement in the East—Second Impression*, 1962, Moscow, pp. 14 –15.

look to your verdict and see whether you have judged right or not—I appeal to you not for myself, but in the interest of the cause which I have the honour to represent. It is the cause that is sacred and I doubt not, gentlemen, that He, before whom all of us will have to stand one day to render an account of our actions will inspire you with the courage of your convictions and help you in arriving at a right decision on the issue involved in this case."

The Judge Advocate pleaded for the Crown for more than four hours, referring to his misfortune to sit through Tilak's "ravings from morning to evening". He concluded at 7 p.m. As a special case, the Judge, Mr. Davar, kept the court open. The Jury decided by 7 in favour of convicting and 2 against. The Judge agreed with the Jury. He asked Tilak whether he wished to say anything before sentence was passed. Tilak maintained his innocence, and without a moment's hesitation replied:

- "All I wish to say is that inspite of the verdict of the Jury, I maintain that I am innocent. There are higher powers that rule the destiny of men and nations and it may be the will of Providence that the cause I represent may prosper more by my suffering than by my remaining free."

The Judge sentenced him to six years transportation, plus a fine of Rs. 1000. The police rushed him to Sabarmati Jail, where Tilak celebrated his 53rd birthday, which fell on July 23, 1908. He was removed to Mandlay in Burma, then a province of India (it was separated from India in 1935). His sentence later was commuted to simple imprisonment. In the appeal, the High Court remitted the fine. The news of his arrest spread like wild fire. Bazars were closed, schools and colleges were deserted, mill workers went on strike for six days. Sixteen men fell a victim to police atrocities. Tilak was treated like a common convict, which attracted questions even in the British Parliament. Sir Henry Cotton said that he must be treated like a political prisoner and that the treatment meted out to him was harsh indeed. The British Government released Tilak only after he had virtually completed his six years' deportation. Gopal Krishna Gokhale was a political opponent of Tilak. Gokhale's detractors alleged that Gokhale was behind Tilak's prosecution. Referring to this, Gokhale stated in one of his letters to his friend:

> "I felt strongly that I owed it not merely to myself and those who were associated with me, but also to public life in India that the miserable miscreants who made it their business to sit down deliberately and concoct malignant falsehood against me and others must not be left severely alone any longer; and so I wired to Mr. Dravid to serve lawyer's notices on all such journals as had made or given currency to the dastardly and detestable accusation that I was at the bottom of Mr. Tilak's prosecution."

Earlier in 1897, he had been sentenced to 18 months' imprisinment, as the Government resented his political activities. Even a moderate like Surendra Nath Banerjee had said about his incarceration, "Whole nation is in tears."

During the Home Rule Movement in 1916, Tilak was again charged for sedation, but was not convicted. Possibly, the British feared reaction in the Army, which had large contingents of the Marathas.

The fact remains that Tilak, throughout his long political career, reverined defiant of the imperial power. The authorities could not break him. Oppression made him bolder and a living martyr. His concept of "Swaraj" became a reality when India shook off the shackles of slavery and became a free sovereign country.

The shock of the death of Tilak, a titan of freedom struggle, reverborated beyond the frontiers of India. It was a world event. For his country, India, an epoch had ended. India had miles to go. Persons like Gandhi and Nehru took up his unfinished work.

9

NON-COOPERATION CUM SWADESHI MOVEMENT—1920–22

The year 1919 had opened its toll with Jallianwala massacre. The following year 1920 was also pregnant with most significant events. Shortly after Tilak's death on August 1, 1920, Gandhiji's Non-cooperation-cum-Swadeshi agitation was launched. In order, to fully appreciate the historic role of Gandhiji and the Congressmen in this struggle, it is perhaps necessary to go into some details of the constituents which were welded into his own movement by Gandhiji—viz., the Khilafat and the Akali movements which were merged in his Non-Cooperation Campaign.

THE KHILAFAT MOVEMENT

ALI BROTHERS

The Amritsar Session of the Congress had ended with a grand reception of Maulana Shaukat Ali and Mohammad Ali, popularly called 'Ali Brothers'. They had just been released from Chhindwara jail in the Central Provinces. The Muslims in India suspected that the British Government was departing from the earlier assurance given to the Muslim by Lloyd George during the

Great War 1914–18 that in the event of Turkey being defeated, she would not be dismembered and places sacrosanct to Islam in the Arab lands would continue to remain in the possession of the Caliph of Turkey. After the War, Britain seemed to finish off Turkey and seize her territories in Palestine, Egypt and elsewhere. The Muslims, in India formed a Khilafat Committee dominated by Ali Brothers to plead with the British authorities in India and abroad. This gave rise to the Khilafat movement. Political atmosphere had become tense with Jallianwala massacre. Its hair raising became fully known on 25th March, 1920, when the Report of the Enquiry Committee set up by the Congress came out. This coincided with the strong Muslim emotions outraged in the Khilafat issue. The British Government was indifferent to the reaction of the Muslims. Gandhiji successfully persuaded the Khilafat leaders including Ali Brothers to join his non-cooperation movement and had thereby quickly seized the opportunity to weld this movement into his own on the basis of common wrongs on the Muslims, the massacre of Jallianwala followed by untold atrocities on Indians and the unsatisfactory British reaction reflected in the Montford Report. Gandhiji concluded:

- "These acts constitute a complete series of wrongs against India which if India had any sense of honour, she must fight at the sacrifice of all the material wealth she possesses; if she does not, she will have bartered her soul for a mess of porridge."[1]

It is significant that Gandhiji gave first priority to Khilafat grievance. Gandhiji felt that such 'an opportunity for uniting Hindus and Mohammadans would not arise in hundred years.[2] Gandhiji had carefully planned the non-cooperation movement and his mastery of execution it became a part of history. Gandhiji started movement with an All India tour in which Ali Brothers accompanied him. They called upon the people to boycott British goods, British courts, Government schools and colleges. Titles conferred by British Sovereign and Government were to be renounced. Politicians were

---

[1] D.G. Tendulkar, '*Mahatma*', Vol. I, p. 291.
[2] Coupland, '*The Indian Problem*', p. 73.

advised to boycott elections to legislatures set up under the Govt. of India Act, 1919. The boycott of colleges, courts and council was hailed as 'Triple Boycott'. The whole of India was in the grip of a stir. Bonfires were made of foreign goods in cities, towns and in the villages from the shores of the Indian ocean upto the farthest hamlet on the high Himalayas, from tha Arakans to Baluchistan and the N.W.F.P.

Pt. Malviya, the nationalist leader, suggested to Gandhiji to have his movement sanctioned by A.I.C.C. Gandhiji retorted:

- " If I am in a minority, I may not pursue my policy in the name of the Congress. The decision of the Congress on any given question, therefore, does not mean that it prevents a Congressman from any action to the contrary, but of the acts, he does so at his own risk and with the knowledge that the Congress is not with him."[3]

However, Gandhiji saw the legitimate validity of this suggestion and had his movement properly endorsed at the Special Session at Calcutta (1920). The movement was a successful challenge to the British Government and thousands participated in it irrespective of religion or region. They suffered torture, jail, confiscation of property and untold atrocities.

THE AKALI AGITATION FOR THE CONTROL OF GURDWARAS IN PUNJAB—1920 -25

The non-cooperation campaign of the Congress under Gandhiji had successfully absorbed the Khilafat agitation welded together the principal communities in the nationalist cause. The Congress similarly blessed agitation of the Akalis directed towards popular control of Gurdwaras in the Punjab. The issue came up in 1920, when a conflict developed between the Mahants or hereditary managers of Sikh shrines and endowments. Many of the Mahants misused the funds offered in the Sikh shrines by the devotees or the income derived from endowments. Claims and counter claims in law

[3] D.G. Tendulkar, '*Mahatma*', Vol. II, pp. 2–3.

courts were time consuming, as legal proceedures were dilatory. The Sikh patriots who had participated in the national non-cooperation campaign had acquired leadership of the Sikhs reformers. They formed Jathas, or militant volunteer groups, calling themselves the Akalis. They were then patriotic Indians and non-fundamentalists. The Punjab administration having tasted the disaffection caused by Jallianwala massacre was now more careful in dealing with the agitation. On 20 February, 1920, the Akalis, who were fully supported by the Indian National Congress, marched on Nankana Sahib, the holiest shrine of the Sikhs (now located in Pakistan). The Mahants' Pathan retainers massacred or lynched some 130 Akalis. The administration favoured the obscurantist Mahants and began to arrest, lathi-charge or shoot the Akali Jathas. As a result, this became a mass movement. Gandhiji, Malviyaji and top Congress leaders blessed the movement. Jawaharlal Nehru, then a young emerging nationalist, got himself arrested and suffered incarceration in jail in this cause. The movement contained well known nationalist Congressmen like Baba Kharak Singh, who sacrificed a lucrative legal practice in the cause. Agreement with Government on legislation was difficult, as the British rulers had opted to support vested interests. It was after a long struggle, which involved barbaric oppression of the populace by an irresponsible foreign executive that at long last a bill was enacted in 1925 vesting control of Gurdwaras located in Punjab in an elected body of the Sikhs, namely Shiromani Gurdwara Prabandhak Committee. Subsequently, the leadership changed hands.

The non-cooperation-Swadeshi movement of Gandhiji in which he had planted the Khilafat and Akali movements had established Gandhiji's credentials as a great organiser. Men like the Nehrus (father and son), Malviya, Ali Brothers, in fact all eminent Indians looked to him for guidance. Jinnah and the moderates adopted the alibi of confining themselves to constitutional methods and kept out of the movement. Gandhiji had now successfully stepped in to fill the vacuum of Tilak's death and he took initiatives in mobilising public opinion against the Raj on a scale hitherto unprecedented. A few years after Tilak's death, when Gandhiji visited Ratnagiri in 1927, the birth place of Tilak, he specifically referred to

Tilak's request "Swaraj is my Birth Right". Gandhiji said, "I do not think there is any follower of the Lokamanya who has tried to carry out his Mantra (Swaraj is my birth right) more than I have."[4]

[4] D.G. Tendulkar, '*Mahatma*', Vol. III, p. 262.

10

THE STORMY YEARS

SPECIAL SESSION—1920 AT CALCUTTA

A special session of the Congress was held in Calcutta from 4th to 9th September, 1920 under the presidentship of Lala Lajpat Rai. Lalaji in his address said:

- "I believe in a righteous and stern and unyielding struggle. I am quite perpared for defeats and repulses. The political principles which I believe in very strongly, are, that nations are by themselves made, it is righteousness that exalts a nation."

Resolution on the death of Lokmanya Bal Ganga Dhar Tilak, Punjab wrongs, condemning Hunter's Committee Report on Punjab were adopted. Main resolution on Khilafat wrongs was moved by Gandhiji himself.

THIRTY-FIFTH SESSION—1920 AT NAGPUR

This session was presided over by Mr. Vijayaraghavachariar. In his address he said:

- "We have to send this message to our sovereign that the people of India are now placed by their rulers in an intolerable position and that they are determined forthwith to make their beautiful country fit and safe for their sons and daughters to live in, and that any further delay in their achievement of this vital object means ruin to them and peril to the Empire if not to the future peace of the world. I would make an earnest appeal to you to realise that the crisis has now reached its worst and this session may be rightly termed to be 'the Thermopylae' in the history of India, certainly in the history of Indian National Congress. I venture to think that our fate just now lies chiefly in the hands of two men, the Rt. Hon'ble Mr. Montague and Mahatmaji.

This session was a personal triumph of Gandhiji and he received full support from leaders like Shri Deshbandhu Chitranjan Das (CR) and Lala Lajpat Rai.

Non-cooperation movement resolution of Calcutta was reaffirmed. It was decided to promote Tilak Memorial Fund and also to boycott the forthcoming visit of Duke of Connaught.

A delegation of Labour Party of England also attended the session and conveyed Labour Party's greetings and sympathy.

THIRTY-SIXTH SESSION—1921 AT AHMEDABAD

This session was presided over by Hakim Ajmal Khan of Delhi in the absence of Shri C.R. Das who was arrested before the session. Hakim Sahib paid glowing tribute to Shri C.R. Das and said:

- "He has done greater service to his country by this arrest than he would probably have done by presiding over."

Some of the extracts from Shri C.R. Das's undelivered speech are:

- "I cannot accept the fundamental principle on which the Reforms Act is based. Freedom is inherent in every nation, and India has and possesses the right to develop her own individuality, and to evolve her own destiny unhampered by what the British Parliament has decided or may decide for us. Any power that hampers or embarasses the attainement of this aim is an enemy of India and must as such be resisted.

- "Freedom is my birth right and I demand a recognition of that right not by instalments nor in compartments but whole and entire."

This session appointed Mahatma Gandhi as its sole executive authority and vested all powers of the All India Congress and confirmed same powers on his successors in the case of his arrest

THIRTY-SEVENTH SESSION—1922 AT GAYA

This session was presided over by Deshbandhu Chitranjan Das. He said:

- "I am not against the boycott of Councils. I am simply of the opinion that the system of Reformed Councils with their steel-frame of the Indian Civil Service are absolutely unsuited to India."
- "There is no royal road to Freedom and difficult and dark will be the path leading to it. Anger is not for you. For you is the hope of dawn and the confidence of the morning."

The main question which was supermost and created excitement and differences among delgates, was the question of councils entry. Pandit Motilal Nehru and Sriniwas Iyengar were for the council entry, overwhelming majority of delgates was against. Boycott of councils was confirmed.

Akali's peaceful and non-violent struggle for Gurdwara Reforms was highly appreciated.

THIRTY-EIGHTH SESSION—1923 AT CALCUTTA

This session was presided over by Maulana Mohammed Ali. In this session doubts about the Boycott programme adopted at Delhi, were clarified. It affirmed that the principle and policy of boycott remained unaltered.

This session also decided to form an All India Volunteer Organisation and an All India Khadi Board.

It was also decided to send Smt Sarojini Naidu and Mr. George Joseph as its delgates to Kenya Indian Congress. Congress also resolved to stand by Sikhs in their struggle for Gurdwara Reforms.

THIRTY-NINTH SESSION—1924 AT BELGAUM

This session was presided over by Mahatma Gandhi. Gandhiji in his address said:

- "From the September of 1920 the Congress has been principally an institute for developing strength from within. It has ceased to function by means of resolutions addressed to the Government for redress of grievances. It did so because it ceased to believe in the beneficial character of the existing system of Government."

He explained his opinion on non-cooperation as means of attaining political freedom, and boycott of foreign cloth. As regards Khadi, he said:

- "I have no better or other message than that of spinning wheel (charkha & takli) for the nation. I know no other effective method for the attainment of Swaraj if it is to be by peaceful and ligitimate means. It is the only substitute for violence, that can be accepted by the whole nation. I would strive for Swaraj within the Empire but would not hesitate to sever connections if severance became a necessity through Britain's own fault."

As regards Swaraj Party formed by Pt. Motilal Nehru and others against the policy of the Congress said, "The Swaraj Party represents, if not a majority, at least a strong and growing and minority in the Congress."

Congress franchise was altered. All elected members of the Congress Committees were required to send 2000 yards of hand spun yarn every month.

FORTIETH SESSION—1925 AT KANPUR

This session was presided over by Smt. Sarojni Naidu. She said:

- "You having elected me, at so grave an hour, of the nation's history, have done something that throughout centuries may serve to redeem for one moment the shame and degradation of your fallen manhood, in giving to a mere

SMT. SAROJINI NAIDU

woman, the woman who for years and years, rocked the cradle and sung lullaby to that national standard which is the emblem of your own regenration, you have gone back to the earliest inspiration that built your civilisation and admitted the woman a co-sharer and a comrade in the secular and spiritual evolution of a people. I, weak and unworthy though be, am of that spiritual descent that has for mothers the purity of Sita, the courage of Savitri and faith of Damyanti and having this for ancestry the meanest woman becomes consecrated, perhaps by traditions to serve and succour her land."

- "Where shall I find the language, where shall I find that living-fire that shall kindle in your hearts an undying fire ? How shall I stir your hearts ! How shall I light that flame that cannot die so that your slavery, so that your disunion, so that all the things that make you hungry and naked and forlorn, oppressed and battered shall be burnt in that undying fire."
- "In the battle for liberty fear is the one unforgivable treachery and despair the one unforgivable sin."

Resolutions reaffirming faith in Civil Disobedience, propagation of Khadi, support to the office of Swarajist and to Government were adopted.

Rev. J.H. Holmes an American addressed the session, wearing a Gandhi cap. He said:

- "I claim Gandhiji for the whole world."
- "The Society of Friends which I represent regards him (Gandhiji) with great reverence and has full belief in his work. I ought to say that we have gone very far in the pursuit for wealth and power. It is a deep evil in our

whole Western Civilization. Our love for wealth has resulted in its concentration, our longing for power has brought on, war after war, and will like plunge us in further wars, until civilization is destroyed. So we gladly turn to you who indicating another and better way and follow the brotherly spirit which is represented by the great among you."

FORTY-FIRST SESSION—1926 AT GUAHATI

This session was presided over by Mr. S. Sriniwas Iyengar. In his address he said:

- "The foremost of our duties, for the coming years is to mobilise all our forces on the issue of National Demand which was formulated in February, 1924 by Pt. Motilal Nehru on behalf of the Nationalist Party consisting of Swarajists and Independents. It asked the Government to establish full responsible Government in India and for that purpose to summon at an early date a representative Round Table Conference."

Resolution on the murder of Swami Shardhanand was moved by Gandhiji and seconded by Maulana Mohammad Ali.

Congress asked the Congressmen in the Councils:

1. Not to accept ministerships.
2. To throw out all proposals proposed by the Government.
3. Not to pass budget.

Habitual wearing of Khadi was made essential for Congressmen holding positions in the organisation.

11

PARLIAMENTARY EXPERIMENT

In the early struggle for liberation of the country several eminent and devoted leaders of the Indian National Congress had extensive experience of parliamentary life. They made notable contribution to the legislative process. Among them could be included men like Gokhale, Madan Mohan Malviya, Lala Lajpat Rai, Motilal Nehru, C.R. Das and lot of others.

In 1922–23, an All India Congress Committee met at Lucknow. It appointed the 'Civil Disobedience Inquiry Committee' to report on the political position in the country and assess possibility of starting of civil disobedience. The Committee included Motilal Nehru, Hakim Ajmal Khan, C. Raja-Gopalachari, Mukhtiar Ahmed Ansari, Vithalbhai Patel and Kasturiranga Aiyangar. The said Civil Disobedience Enquiry Committee concluded that the time was not ripe for Civil Disobedience. On the question of Council entry, the Committee was not of one mind. Hakim Ajmal Khan, Motilal Nehru and Vithalbhai Patel favoured entry in the legislatures to wreck the constitution from within. Other did not favour it. Both sections were strongly patriotic.

Finally C.R. Das resigned as President of the Congress. He announced formation of Swaraj Party within the Congress (January, 1923). The British had engineered Hindu-Muslim riots. In the meanwhile, with the assumption of political power by Kamal Ataturk replacing the Caliph in Turkey, the Khilafat movement had lost its relevance The Swaraj Party gradually became a strong group. On his release from jail, Lala Lajpat Rai, the Lion of Punjab also joined this group. The Swarajists were elected members of the legislature in the states and at the Centre but they only functioned as opposition leaders there.

In the Central Assembly in Delhi, the leader of the Congress Party, Shri Motilal Nehru had a difficult task, as substantive political power rested with the Viceroy's Executive Council. But Motilal Nehru was endowed with most distinguished abilities and proved his mettle. He was able to register a victory for his party in the Central Assembly, when his motion demanding a 'Round Table Conference' to have full Responsible Government in India was carried out by 76 against 48 votes, despite strong opposition from the official side. He repeated his performance, to the chagrin of official benches, on some other important occasions also. He was ably assisted by Vithalbhai Patel who in a spirited speech on budget estimates recalled the evils of the British Raj over a century, protesting against the arrest of 30,000 to 40,000 people during the non-cooperation movement. He warned the Government, "Unless you are prepared to mend your ways and to come to terms with us, the Treasury Benches will no longer remain a bed of roses."

While the Swarajists under Motilal Nehru were offering patriotic resistance to the rulers in various legislatures, Gandhiji was released on 5th February, 1924 following an operation of appendicitis on him. The Swarajists and the section led by Gandhiji had some differences on the Council entry. However, their relations remained most cordial. Later on Gandhiji complimented Motilal Ji. "There is no doubt that the Swarajists have created a stir in the Government circles. There is no doubt that any withdrawal at the moment will be misunderstood as a rout and weakness."[1] Motilal Nehru expressed his surprise on Gandhiji's encouraging observations. Gandhiji then added, "it would be disastrous if the Swarajists retired from the Council." The differences were, thus, resolved fully.

Hindu-Muslim riots engineered by the British continued right upto 1925. Gandhiji began a fast of 21 days at the

[1] D.G. Tendulkar, *'Mahatma'*, pp. 140 –145.

residence of Maulana Mohammad Ali. This somewhat relieved the situation.

Gandhiji's fasts, as political weapon, have a unique place in modern history. However, he owns no exclusive primative on this technique. Mr. Swirey, the Irish patriot hard fasted himself unto death in the British prison at Brixton in Dec. 1920. His dying words were "It is not those who inflict the most, but those who suffer the most will conquer."[2] The Indian patriot Jitender Das similarly fasted himself to death in the prison at Lahore in 1929 and his fight against the Raj did not go in vain.

Deshbandhu C.R. Das suddenly expired on 16th June, 1925 at Darjeeling. Secretary of State, Birkenhead made a notorious anti-India speech on 10th July, 1925 which again united all sections of the Congress. Gandhiji now initiated the All India Spinners's Association and expressed the view that there was ample scope for both the constructive programme and Council entry.

On 22nd August, 1925, Vithalbhai Patel, the veteran Congress leader, was elected President of the Central Assembly. When his predecessor Sir Frederick Whyte invited him to take the chair, Patel is stated to have whispered Mr. Jumna Das who was sitting nearby, "Let the scoundrels see what happens."[3] He was a tough guy and informed the Viceroy that the convention which allowed the Viceroy to address the House in the Assembly Chamber was grossly derogatory to the Chair. He insisted that whenever the Viceroy was to speak to the Assembly, he must come to Patel's chamber. Several high dignitaries pleaded with Patel, but he did not relax. The Viceroy came from the back door of Vithalbhai's Chamber and all pomp and ceremony attending the Viceroy's arrival disappeared.[4]

Indian National Congress candidates participated in ensuing elections in 1926 for the Central and provincial legislatures. However, a section under Pt. Madan Mohan Malviya and Lala Lajpat Rai formed the Indian National Party to

---

[2] Padraig O' Malley, '*The Uncivil wars—Ireland Today*', 1983; Belfast UK; p. 266.

[3] Goverdhanbhai Patel, '*Vithalbhai Patel*', Vol. II, p. 653.

[4] *Ibid*, p. 718.

oppose the Congress. Once within the legislature, both groups cooperated on many issues. While Congressmen were exposing the British misrule from within the legislatures, their colleagues outside the legislatures were also waging an effective fight to dislodge the British from political power in South Asia.

FORTY-SECOND SESSION—1927 AT MADRAS

This session was presided over by Dr. Mukhtiar Ahmed Ansari. In his address he said:

- "Indians do not claim anything more or less than that they shall occupy the same position, and enjoy the same rights in their country as free people do in their own."
- "Once India is free the whole edifice of Imperialism will collapse as this is the keystone of the arch Imperialism."

How prophetic these words were?

12

ALL PARTIES CONFERENCE

NEHRU REPORT

An All Parties Conference was convened in British India in Feb–March, 1928 with a view to determine the principles for devising a Constitution for an Indian dominion. In August, 1928 Motilal Nehru and Tej Bahadur Sapru presented details of such a constitution which came to be known as the Nehru Report. The report proposed, inter-alia, that with reference to the Indian States, the new Indian Dominion would have the same rights and obligations towards the princely states arising from the treaties as were exercised and discharged by the Government of India.[1]

Jawaharlal Nehru and the radical wing of the Indian National Congress resented that the Nehru Report pleaded for only dominion status, instead of full independence. Gandhiji now intervened and brought about a reconciliation. However, at the next session this question was considered in greater details.

FORTY-THIRD SESSION—1928 AT CALCUTTA

This session was presided over by Pandit Motilal Nehru. Following are some of the extracts from his address.

- "Non co-operation followed Dyerism and O'Dwyerism. The great giant i.e. India woke up for a while and the very

[1] C.H. Philips, *Evolution of India and Pakistan*: Selected documents 1962, London; p. 233.
S.R. Ashton, *British Policy towards the Indian State*; Select Books Service Syndicate, (1985); New Delhi, p. 123.

awakening shook, the foundation of British rule. There was a reaction and a relapse but again we are on the threshold of another great struggle for freedom.

- "I wish to urge that the country should lose no time in preparing itself for the next move forward. I urge that all energies and resources be concentrated on fighting the enemy residing inside our body politic, viz. communal and political discord."
- "The work before the young and old is one and the same. My humble services, for what they are worth, are at your disposal. Let us sink our differences. Let us march forward shoulder to shoulder and victory is ours."

Another event of the year was success of Barodoli Satyagraha under the leadership of Vallabhbhai Patel and Gandhiji honoured Patel with title of 'Sardar'. From that day he was known as Sardar Patel.

Usual resolution for the boycott of foreign cloth and British goods, and propagation of Khadi were adopted.

The main resolution of the session was an ultimatum to British Government to accept All Parties Committees Report by 31st December, 1929, failing which the goal of the Congress would be Complete Independence. Mrs. Annie Besant said that it was a dignified and clear statement on India's goal.

13

THE SIMON COMMISSION—1927–28

Congressmen, particularly Gandhiji, Motilal Nehru and Lala Lajpat Rai, felt deeply concerned about the denial of substantive political rights to Indians. There was a strong and growing desire among the Indian leaders that the British Government ought to define formally a self government of the type enjoyed by the Dominions as India's constitutional goal. Jawaharlal Nehru, Subhash Bose and their young followers were, however, vociferous in their demand for full independence and restoration of unabridged sovereignty to India. The Indian public was much exercised on discrimination against Indians in the Dominions and with regard to their inferior status in the world community as a subject people. Men like Pandit Malviya reminded people of their proud inheritance and how the Indian people were courting serfdom imposed by the foreign rulers. The demand for liberalisation of the constitution for Government of India could no longer be resisted.

Successive British Government adopted the alibi of instituting statutory Commissions as a part of 'gradual transfer of power', but the British Government lacked sincerity and projected only sham expectations. British bureaucrats, specially officers of the Indian Political Service, were most reluctant to part with power. They maneuvered invariably to deny any real share to Indians in the art of government of their own country. Yet, the demand for liberalisation of constitutional set-up could not be indefinitely ignored in spite of efforts of the ruling foreign government to create discord between the majority community and the Muslims minority. This they did by engineering communal riots on frivolous grounds. The agents provocateurs were bribed or patronised. Even the Hindu intelligensia was sought to be subdivided so that the Raj may rest safe and secure.

The Government of the United Kingdom announced on 8th November, 1927 appointment of a Parliamentary Commission, headed by Sir John Simon to suggest constitutional revisions for the Government of India. Members of the said statutory Commission were all of them 'Seven Good Englishmen', to quote a phrase of Stanley Baldwin. Representation by any Indian member was thereby extinct. Total exclusion of Indians was strongly resented. This was a deliberate insult to the self respect of the Indian Nation. No one could swallow this bitter pill of humiliation. The announcement caused unprecedented discontent and disaffection against the 'Raj'. The Indian National Congress, cognizant of the strong national feeling on this issue, announced a boycott of the 'Simon Commission'. The National Party, the Liberal Federation, the Hindu Mahasabha and the Jinnah faction of the Muslim League were one on this sensitive matter.

The personnel of the Commission consisted of imperialist 'hardliners'. Mr. Richard Clement Attlee (later Prime Minister responsible for transfer of power to the truncated India) too was inducted in Commission only for his known image, at the time, of being a 'conservative among the Labourites". Other Commissioners enjoyed no greater reputation, while as a scholar at the Hailebury and Imperial College, young Attlee was considered "He was pleased with romantic ideas about the imperial authority of Great Britain" and "intoxicated by a vision of large portions of the school map coloured in red with people ruled for their own good by strong, silent men, civil servants and soldiers as portrayed by Kipling." Later years brought him maturity. He joined the Labour Parliamentary Party and, in course of time, by a freak of history (he superseded elder party men) became the leader of the party. In the capacity of the Prime Minister of Great Britain he acted a crucial role in the transfer of power in 1947 to the partitioned India. However, the future liberator and divisor Clement Attlee was treated with rest of his fellow commissioners with contumely by the Indian Press. The 'National

Herald' reported, "Mr. Attlee cut a very sorry figure when tackled by the press people. . . . He was asked what was the significance of the Labour War Lords being chosen to represent Labour on the Commission; Major Attlee was so flabbergasted by the volley of questions that his hand began to shiver as he tried to light his pipe. The press men thought it cruel to bully him any more, and as they were taking leave of him, the Major said, Thank You.[1] Attlee even did not consider resigning his Commission, when the principal Indian political parties had boycotted the Simon Commission, as it was "All White" and "Discriminatory". After many years, Attlee argued that, in spite of their apparent suppression, the Simon proposals were essentially those under which India was ruled until after the war.[2]

This was too simplistic a view.

The socalled Simon Commission landed in Bombay on 3rd February, 1928, but was greeted by an all India strike of workers, politicians, academicians alike.

Bombay witnessed a mammoth procession shouting "SIMON GO BACK". In Delhi, Allahabad and other cities the Commission had similar experience of being greeted by boycott, black flags and indignant public reaction.

In the Central Assembly, the Lion of Punjab, Lala Lajpat Rai moved a resolution on 16th February, 1928 calling upon the Governor-General in Council to convey to his Home Government in U.K. "the Assembly's entire lack of confidence in the Parliamentary Commission which has been appointed to review the Constitution of India". He asserted that 'the problem of India in its relation with England was not a problem for any Commission of Enquiry'. In the Assembly, members including M.A. Jinnah, expressed strong resentment to the Secretary of State, Lord Birkenhead's speech, dated 10th July, 1927, whereby his lordship had questioned fitness of Indians for self-government. In the resumed dabate on 18th February, 1928, Mr. Motilal Nehru, commenting on Lord Birkenhead's ill conceived speech, stated, "heads that are

---

[1] William Golant; *The Long Afternoon—British India (1601–1947)*, Vikas Publishers, (1976), Delhi, pp. 115–117.

[2] Attlee, C.R.: *As it happeed*, 1954. London.

swollen contain little wisdom and that a man who rides high, rides for a fall". He warned the Imperial Government in prophetic words, ". . . . What has not been accomplished by the statesmanship of England, will be accomplished by the people, adding another to the number of fallen empires." Madan Mohan Malviya roared "that Lord Birkenhead was a big bully who would drive Indians further from their English fellow subject" and emphasized that "unless the King Emperor appointed an equal number of Indians we refuse to cooperate." Lajpat Rai's resolution was carried by a majority vote.

The cost on "Simon Commission" came up for discussion, when the budget estimates, were considered by the Central Assembly. Pt. Motilal Nehru's cut motion rejecting the budget demand concerning the Commission was passed by 66 against 59 votes in the Central Assembly. This caused lot of harassment to the Viceroy, who had to exercise the Veto.[3]

Hostile demonstrations, involving serious incidents, greeted the Simon Commission, particularly in Lahore and Lucknow. In Lahore, Lala Lajpat Rai was assaulted with some of his followers. He was a sick man. The police assault on Lalaji caused severe injuries, which resulted in his martyrdom on 17th November, 1928. According to an eye witness Raizada Lala Hansraj, Lajpat Raiji ordered the procession to stop, when it reached the barricades raised by the Police. Yet, the Senior Superintendent of Police, Mr. Scott hurled blows with his stick on Lalaji. Lala Duli Chand and Mr. K. Santhaman, who tried to ward off blows on Lala Lajpat Raiji received lathi blows. Later on, Lalaji declared that "every blow on my body is a nail in the coffin of the British Empire". This eventually proved prophetic.

In Lucknow, Jawaharlal Nehru and Pandit Govind Ballabh Pant had a similar experience. In the Central Assembly Motilal Nehru stated:

- "It was he, who was attacked not from one side, but from three sides, and had he not been surrounded by his young followers he could not possibly have been left alive. I am

---

[3] D.P. Mishra, *Living an Era*, Vikas Publishers, Delhi, pp. 115–118.

making no charge. I do not care nor does the boy care". Besides Jawaharlal Nehru, Govind Ballabh Pant, the leader of the Congress Party in the Local Council, and they both came in for countless attacks. I saw both of them and they appeared just as a painter had painted them block and blue all over their bodies, but they are both young and strong men, and they made light of these serious injuries."

- "The cowardly attacks on Lala Lajpat Rai and other nationalist leaders created a wave of disaffection. A section of young people including Bhagat Singh rowed to avenge his martyrdom. This led to murder of Saunders, a British Sergeant in Lahore, when patriotic terrorists mistook for the nefarious Scott. Bhagat Singh, Rajguru and Sukhdev were arrested later on and hanged in Lahore Central Jail on 23rd March, 1931. Gandhiji's mediation with the Viceroy did not succeed in saving the lives of these proud and unrepentent patriots. Lord Irwin might have relented on the question, but for unanimous opposition by Provincial Governors led by imperialist Malcolm Hailey."

14

INDEPENDENCE—THE CONGRESS GOAL

FORTY-FOURTH SESSION—1929 AT LAHORE

This session was presided over by Pt. Jawaharlal Nehru.

PT. JAWAHARLAL NEHRU

Some of the extracts from his address are:

- "Brick by brick has our national movement been built up and often on the prostrate bodies of her martyred sons India has advanced. The giants of old may not be with us but the courage of old is with us still and India can yet produce martyrs like Jatindra and Vijaya. The brief day of European domination is already approaching its end."
- "I must frankly confess that I am a Socialist and a Republican and am no believer in Kings and Princes or in the order which produces the modern Kings of industry who have greater powers over the lives and fortunes of men than even Kings of old whose methods are predatory as those of the old feudal aristocracy."
- "We have now an open conspiracy to free this country from foreign rule and all our countrymen and country-

women are willing to join it. But the rewards that are in store for you are suffering and prison and it may be death."

Among the resolutions adopted were, deploring bomb outrage on the Viceroy's train, boycott of Round Table Conference, boycott of future elections to the legislature, and declaring Complete Independence as goal of the Congress.

Minorities were assured that no solution of future constitution would be acceptable to the Congress which did not give full satisfaction to the minorities.

Pandit Jawaharlal Nehru unfurled the Congress Flag on New Year's Day, 1930 at the banks of River Ravi amidst shouts of 'Inqilab Zindabad'.

It was decided to celebrate 26th January, 1930 as Independence Day throughout the country.

HISTORIC SIGNIFICANCE OF LAHORE DECLARATION: NEHRU'S POLITICAL PHILOSOPHY

Jawaharlal Nehru had the rare privilege of succeeding his father as Congress President. He had successfully piloted the Independence Declaration Resolution in Madras Session 1927 and re-emphasised that Congress goal was to attain full Independence for the country at Lahore Session. According to Mohan Lal Saxena, a close associate of Pt. Motilal Nehru and later, a minister in the Union Cabinet under Pandit Jawaharlal Nehru, the credit to mould the personality of Jawaharlalji went to a great extent to his great father. He adds:

- "Somehow, Pandit Motilal had presaged the role which his unusual child Jawahar was destined to play or he himself desired him to play, so, from the beginning he tried to inculcate in his son high principles, good habits, a broad outlook, catholic approach and above all courage and capacity for hard work, which characterised Jawaharlal and enabled him to serve his country so well. But he never allowed his great love for the son to come in the way of his duties as a father. Even when Jawaharlal was studying abroad he did not relax this grip."[1]

[1] Kumar, Nand: *Wither Freedom*. Letters and Writings of Mohan Lal Saxena, pp. 195 –196.

When the young Nehru was elected Congress President of the Lahore Ṣession (1929) Motilalji made it a point to go to Lahore and stay there for a week.

He witnessed that the President-elect, young Jawaharlal, riding on a horse back was taken out in a grand procession. It was for the first time that a son took over from his father the highest office then in the gift of the nation. The happy anḍ proud parents watched the Presidential procession from a balcony in Anarkali. Much later, after India became free, Smt. Indira Gandhi, the illustrious daughter of Jawaharlal Nehru too became the Congress President in 1959. Referring to the filial affection between father, Motilal Nehru and his son Jawaharlal, Mohan Lal Saxena adds:

- "When they were in jail together, Jawahar Lal took great pains to make jail life less irksome for his ailing father. A few months before his death, the father wrote from Naini Jail to his daughter, "As it is, everything is found for me and I have nothing to do but to eat, sleep and read Hari, his valet (who died in 1961) should do well to take a leaf out of Jawahar's book in the matter of serving me. . . . He anticipates everything and leaves nothing for me to do. I wish there were many fathers to boast of such sons."[2]

Jawaharlal's address at the Lahore Session was a unique challenging declaration. It served the historic notice of the Indian National Congress on the foreign Government that the unjust alien political order must go. His thoughts on socialism support to anticolonial forces on a global scale, love for democracy which in due course became the hall mark of the Constitution of free India were the concepts which materialised Nehru's thinking. Thus, the address reflected broad humanism and a micro-view of Nehru's political philosophy which proved of inestimable value to modern India.

His address proclaimed his political manifesto promising socialism, secularism and democracy for his country and justice to all without distinction of sex, caste, colour or creed. It became the bed-rock on which new India could seek a safe, secure and strong foundation.

---

2. Kumar, Nand: *Wither Freedom*. Letters and Writings of Mohan Lal Saxena, pp. 195 –196.

15

CIVIL DISOBEDIENCE—1930

The substantive part of the Lahore Congress resolution demanding complete Independence related to starting of Civil Disobedience on a massive scale. Authority for this was vested in the All India Congress Committee. However, practically speaking, it was Mahatma Gandhi who decided the future course of action. The poet Rabindra Nath Tagore met him at Sabarmati Ashram where Gandhiji was then staying. It was probably 18th January, 1930. The poet asked the Mahatma about the action he proposed to undertake against the British Govt. Gandhiji was not yet clear about it and is stated to have replied, "I do not yet see any light coming out of the surrounding darkness". Yet, his mind was active and he was pondering all the time about the form he should give to his movement. Shortly afterwards, he wrote in "Young India", that "granted a perfectly non-violent atmosphere and a fulfilled constructive programme. I would undertake to lead the mass Civil Disobedience struggle to a successful issue in the space of few months." Later, replying to critics, Gandhiji said, "The Congress cannot stay its hands having passed the Independence resolution. It was no bluff, no showing nothing. It is then as much upto the critics as to me, to devise ways and means of achieving independence."[1]

On being told that his movement might result in Hindu-Muslim clashes, which the British authorities could well have engineered, Gandhiji clarified his thinking in an address to the students of Gujarat Vidyapith and he retorted, "Votary as I am of non-violence, if I was given choice between being a

[1] D.G. Tendulakar, '*Mahatama*' Vol. III, pp. 1–2, 6.

helpless witness to chaos and perpetual slavery, I should unhesitatingly say that I would far rather be witness to Hindus and Muslims doing one another to death than that I should daily witness our gilded slavery."

The atmosphere was, thus, gradually being charged with electric fervour of the impending battle. Throughout India, January 26 the day resolution on Independence was proclaimed, was celebrated in the cities, towns as well as the country side—in the factories, palaces and in the huts. The text of the resolution was read at corner meetings, in market places and in prominent localities to the gathering crowds, without making any speeches. People approved it with a show of hands. The nation was now fully geared for the ensuring crusade against the foreign power. The Indian National Congress had become the fulcrum of revolution.

The Mahatma took the Government of India by surprise, when he issued abruptly an ultimatum calling upon the authorities to concede to his 11 demands, if they desired him to put off his Civil Disobedience programme. These demands called for (1) total prohibition, (2) restoration of exchange rate to 16 d., (3) 50 per cent reduction in land revenue, (4) abolition of Salt Tax, (5) 50 per cent reduction in the salaries of civil services, (6) 50 per cent reduction in military expenses, (7) a protective tariff against foreign cloth, (8) enactment of a coastal reservation bill, (9) discharge of all political prisoners save those condemned for murder, (10) abolition of the C.I.D., and (11) issue of licences for fire arms for self defence subject to popular control. At that point of time, many a critic failed to appreciate the significance of these basic demands. Much later, Pandit Jawaharlal Nehru wrote[2] that Gandhiji "seemed to emerge from the millions of India, speaking their language and incessantly drawing attention to them and their appalling condition... Get off the back of these peasant and workers who live by their exploitation, got tired of the system that produces this system and misery."

---

[2] Jawaharlal Nehru, *Discovery of India*, p. 358.

THE WAY TO DANDI

On March, 2, 1930 Gandhiji addressed his historic message to the Viceroy through Reginald Reynolds, an Ashram-mate, in which he wrote, "On the eleventh day of the month, I shall proceed with such co-workers of the Ashram, as I can take, to disregard the provisions of the Salt Laws. I regard this tax to be the most iniquitous of all from the poor man's stand point. As the Independence movement is essentially for the poorest in the land the beginning will be made with this evil."[3]

Gandhiji stated *inter alia*:

- "My personal faith is clear, I cannot intentionally hurt anything that lives much less fellow human beings even though they may do the greatest wrong to me, and, in my mind, I hold the British rule in India to be a curse, but I don't therefore consider English men in general to be worse than any other people on earth."

He added:

- "British rule has sapped the foundation of our culture and by the policy of disarmament degraded us spiritually. The resolution of Independence should cause no alarm if the word Dominion Status mentioned in our statement had been used in its accepted sense. What I fear is that there never had been any intention of granting such Dominion Status to India in near future. My ambition is no less than to convert the British people through non-violence. I want to serve them even as I want to serve my own".

He declared further:

- "It is my purpose to set in motion the force of non-violence against the organised violent force of the British rule. This will be expressed through Civil Disobedience. For the moment, it will be confined to the inmates of the

---

[3] D.G. Tendulakar, '*Mahatma*', Vol. III, p. 18.

Satyagrah Ashram, but ultimately designed to cover all those who choose to join the movement."[4]

The Viceroy Lord Irwin argued that the action envisaged was clearly bound to involve violation of the law and danger to public peace. This provoked the Mahatma to say:

- "On bended knees, I asked for bread and received a stone instead. The English nation responds only to force." In a spirited reply to the Viceroy, Gandhiji said, "Instead of the forest of books containing rules and regulations, the only law that the nation knows is the will of the British administration, the only public peace the nation knows is the peace of a public prison. India is one vast prison-house. I repudiate this law, and regard it my sacred duty to break the mournful monotony of the compulsory peace that is choking the heart of the nation for want of free vent."[5]

Gandhiji, for good reason, was not satisfied with the Viceroy's reply nor was he prepared to bow down to the veiled threat held out in the Viceroy's reference to questions of law and public peace. The philosophy of British authorities harboured and generated the sham idea that nationalism could be rolled back by repression.

DANDI MARCH—12TH MARCH, 1930 TO 6TH APRIL, 1930

Faithfully, to the ultimatum, he had delivered to the Government of India, Gandhi announced his campaign, which started on 12th March, 1930. Early morning that day, he held the prayer meeting at 4 a.m. in the open court of the Sabarmati Ashram, received tilak on his forehead and a coconut from his wife, Smt. Kasturba since he was undertaking a non-violent crusade against all the might of the foreign government for liberalisation of his country.

At 6.30 a.m. Gandhiji, stick in hand, clad in dhoti, started on his long march to Dandi—a village on the sea coast of

---

[4] D.G. Tendulakar, '*Mahatma*' Vol. III, pp. 18 –19.
[5] *Ibid.*

Gujarat, accompanied by 78 inmates of his Ashram. He had duly disciplined and trained them for about two years for this very purpose. Being a good judge of men, his selection of the team was judicious. The team included men of probity and sincere patriotism—men like Saint Vinoba Bhave who participated in the march.

The entire journey involved 241 miles (about 400 km) spread over 24 days. To begin with, the itinerary, as initially proposed, would involve five days. In order, however, to make the campaign more effective, Gandhiji decided upon a 24 days' march.

The objective of the march was to seek liberation of India from foreign yoke and as a first step, the hated Indian Salt Act, 1882 was to be defied. Under the provisions of the statute, the British Government had enforced a monopoly on the collection and manufacture of salt, restricting its handling to licensed salt depots subject to a tax levy of Re. 1 and 4 annas per maund (82 lbs.) of salt. Gandhiji and his 78 followers defied the Salt Law on 6th April, 1930 on the sea-shore at Dandi (Gujrat) by simply picking up salt from the beach. But by the time, Gandhi's battalion of non-violent Satyagrahis reached Dandi on 5th April, 1930, India had been shaken to its very depth. At the prayer meeting on 6th April, Gandhiji proclaimed that in the event of his arrest his place would be taken by Abbas Tayabji and then by Sarojini Naidu, the Nightingale of India. At 8.30 a.m. Gandhiji, to quote Mrs. Naidu, became a "Law breaker", when he bent down to pick up a lump of sea salt and held it up in his sacred hand. In a statement, he called upon his compatriots "Now that the technical or ceremonial breach of the Salt Law has been committed, it is open to any one who would take the risk of prosecution under the Salt Law to manufacture salt, where ever he wishes and where ever it is convenient."[6]

Now the entire nation was in motion and a high drama of revolution in the bodies and hearts of men was being enacted all over India to seek freedom from foreign yoke through mass Civil Disobedience by Indians. The Government realised that the small spark set off at Dandi had lit the flame of

[6] D.G. Tendulakar, '*Mahatma*' Vol. III, p. 31.

DANDI MARCH

rebellion on a national scale with a fanfare of global publicity. Thus, initiative had been seized by Gandhiji. By the simple act of manufacturing salt the Congress-men had smashed the British prestige almost in all villages, cities and towns in India.

Before the historic march to Dandi, Sardar Vallabhbhai Patel had been arrested on 7th March, 1930, in Barsad Taluka. He had gone there to prepare the villagers for the reception of Gandhiji and his freedom marchers enroute to Dandi. A protest meeting attended by about 75,000 people was held at Ahmedabad. The participants vowed to follow the path, "where Sardar Patel had gone !" Gandhiji made most of Sardar's arrest and in almost every speech, which he addressed on the way, invoked Sardar Patel's name. Every village gave a rousing reception to him.

Motilal Nehru compared Gandhiji's march to that of 'Rama's march on Lanka.' P.C. Ray compared it to the march of Israelites from Egypt to the SINAE under Moses.' Subhash Bose recalled 'Napoleon march to Paris.' Gandhiji called it a holy pilgrimage, saying that he felt like a pilgrim to Amarnath or Badri-Kedar Nath. He became the "MEHDI" of India's freedom movement.

The Government now resorted to reign of terror. When Gandhiji received tidings of police atrocities, he called the British administration as 'Goonda Raj' and threatened to march, along with his followers, on Dharsana to take possession of the Salt Depot there. Gandhiji protested to the Viceroy, Lord Irwin (later Lord Halifax) that while well known leaders 'were being dealt with more or less according to the legal formality, the rank and file has been often very savagely and in some cases even indecently assaulted.' He called upon the Viceroy to abolish the salt levy or arrest him and "my party unless the country can, as I hope it will, replace every one taken away, by sheer goondaism, unless every head broken is replaced as I hope it will".[7] Gandhiji was arrested on 5th May, 1930, but the Satyagraha continued for over a year until negotiations brought it to an end.

---

[7] D.G. Tendulakar, '*Mahatma*', op cit.; Vol. III, pp. 36 –37.

Gandhiji's countenance on the day of his arrest bore marks of gratified nobility. One may recall the British poet Andre Marvell's lines:

'He nothing common did nor mean
upon that memorable scene !'

Gandhiji had meticulously planned the campaign, studied even meteorological reports to determine the conditions of weather anticipated in the March, suitability of the area to be covered (it lay through Bardoli, where Sardar Patel had successfully executed a Congress campaign earlier) and he had studied experts' reports about grievances of the people of the villages through which his party passed. He carefully planned his speeches and actions enroute to Dandi. He devised himself the marching schedule and rest places to make maximum use of hours between 6 a.m. to 10 p.m. Mass media, including newsmen—Indian and foreign and at least three film companies recognised the dramatic significance of the march to Dandi. Publicity on a global scale was, thus, enabled. Gandhiji's key pronouncements on the way regulated the tempo of the movement. His warnings, administered before the campaign, won him front page coverage in the media the world over and even before the march started every one was on the tiptoe of expectation. Throughout the march, he insisted on maintenance of simple standards of behaviour. In the village of Bhatgram Gandhiji made an impromptu speech, expressing his anguish that some volunteers had ordered milk from Surat to be brought in a motor lorry and they had incurred other expenses which "I could not justify." He added that those who claimed to represent the poor had to live according to their standard. All oscillations and extravagance were to be purged. Volunteers would subsist on common cereal, water, burn candle rather than kerosene, as it was a religious campaign.

As the moment of his victory drew near at Dandi, he poured solid fire on the "Raj" in his speeches. He increased the crescendo of his utterness from day to day. By the beginning of April, the movement had caught on and the British Government had to resort to all kinds of means to suppress it. But the freedom's struggle continued in one or the other form. Gandhi and the Congress had captured the world stage.

Gandhi's triumph as a leader of historic dimension was complete. His spirit can be compared to that of Mowbray in William Shakespeare's King Richard, the Second:

> My honour is my life, both grow in one,
> Take honour from me, and my life is done!

The Dandi March, world's best known non-violent crusade against a mighty empire is without a parallel in human history. One may aptly recall Goldsmith's famous lines :

> "And still they gazed, and still the wonder grew,
> That on small head could carry all he knew !"

The greatest success of Gandhiji lies in the fact, and it will echo through the corridors of centuries, that he took in moral bearings, amid the variety of vice, which is often in the character of a confrontation. He never forgot to preserve the values which in the process could well have been otherwise obscured.

16

GANDHI-IRWIN PEACE PACT 4TH MARCH, 1931

Up to the spring season of 1931, the Congress Civil Disobedience continued. Thousands courted jail, hundreds preferred martyrdom by bullet, and cudgels of a tyrannical police. In N.W.F.P. the veteran associate of Mahatma Gandhi, Khan Abul Ghaffar Khan carried on a non-violent heroic movement against the British rulers. He was popularly acclaimed as the Frontier Gandhi. Subsequently, after India attained freedom, he had the privilege, as a veteran survivor of the Gandhi-Nehru era, to witness the Congress Centenary held at Bombay from 27–30 December, 1985.

But, the veteran leader Pandit Motilal Nehru was gravely ill in jail. He was released a few days earlier to his death, which occurred on 6th February, 1931. At his death bed he prophetically told Gandhiji, "I will not live to see India free, but you shall surely witness the proud day, when she attains Swaraj." His death created a great void. It was the most serious national loss after the death of Tilak and later in June, 1925 that of C.R. Dass.

The terms of the first Round Table Conference convened in London were not found acceptable and the Congress boycotted it. Prime Minister, Ramsay MacDonald, while winding it up significantly observed, "If in the meantime, there is response to the Viceroy's appeal from those engaged at present in Civil Disobedience, and there is a wish to cooperate on the general lines of this delegation, steps will be taken to enlist their services." This was a clear admission of the fact that no settlement of constitutional impasse in India could be reached without the participation of the Indian National Congress, the most representative organisation.

Accordingly, the Viceroy, Lord Irwin opened negotiations with the Congress, which involved a meeting between the Viceroy, representing the Imperial Government and Gandhiji, representing the Indian nation. The negotiations lasted upto the 4th March, 1931 and resulted in what is known as the "Gandhi-Irwin Pact", of 4th March, 1931. Winston Churchill, echoed the views of imperial hard liners, when he reacted, "it is alarming and also nauseating to see Mr. Gandhi, a seditious Middle Temple lawyer, posing as a Fakir of the type well known in the East, standing half naked up the steps of Viceregal Palace, while he is still organising and conducting a defiant campaign of Civil Disobedience, to parley on equal terms with the representative of the King Emperor."[1]

The entire Indian nation was shocked on the hanging of Sardar Bhagat Singh, Rajguru and Sukhdeo on 23 March, 1931, despite Gandhiji's appeal to the Viceroy. At the Karachi Session, the Congress condemned this action of the British Government, but disassociated itself from the policy of violence. This was certainly not liked by most people, as they felt that the Congress should have reacted more strongly to this ghastly act of the imperial power.

In England, the hardliners under Churchill made all out effort to undo the Gandhi Irwin Pact. Under the next Viceroy, Lord Willingdon, a reversal of Irwin's policy was soon to follow.

FORTY-FIFTH SESSION—1931 AT KARACHI

This session was presided over by Sardar Vallabhbhai Patel. This session was held after Gandhi-Irwin Pact. Congressmen attended the session after their release from jail. This was overshadowed with the sorrow and anger due to the execution of Bhagat Singh and his comrades. Youths under the leadership of Subhash Chandra Bose blamed Gandhiji for not doing his best to save these youngmen. The main feature of this session was the adoption of a resolution on Fundamental

[1] D.G. Tendulakar. '*Mahatma*', op cit., Vol. III, p. 53.

Rights, which states: "In order to save the masses from exploitation it is imperative that along with political freedom millions of our masses should also get economic independence in true sense."

17

WILLINGDON TURNS THE WHEEL

Lord Irwin left India on 18th April, 1931, at the end of his tenure as the Viceroy. His successor Lord Willingdon, a former Governor of Bombay, succeeded Lord Irwin. He was hell bent on finishing off the Indian National Congress. He took to a policy of suppression of the nationalist movement and encouraged communal and feudal forces with a view to creating a wedge in the struggle being waged against the Imperial Government.

The Congress on its part, did not take long to discover the design of the new Viceroy and that the hopes created by the Gandhi-Irwin Pact of March 4, 1931 were not to be realised. However, well wishers advised the Congress not to boycott the Second Round Table Conference which was being convened by the British Government in London to consider again the revision of the constitutional set up. As the sole representative of the Indian National Congress, Gandhiji attended the Second said Round Table Conference. Accompanied by Pandit Madan Mohan Malviya, who represented the National Party and Sarojni Naidu, who represented Women of India, Gandhiji sailed for England on 29th August, 1931. The Conference proved of no avail, though Gandhiji was able to meet important British statesmen, including King George in that trip. An interesting account of Gandhiji's meeting with the King Emperor is recorded in the memoirs of Secretary of State Sir Samuel Hoare. Gandhiji refused to observe such protocols as in respect of prescribed dress for a meeting with the King. Gandhiji preferred his Dhoti and refused to put on European dress. This sartorial dead-lock was resolved to Gandhi's satisfaction, since he was exempted from the requirement of court dress precedent to meeting the King. However, both Gandhi and King Geroge V talked amicably. The King warned Gandhi at the end of the meeting, "Mr. Gandhi I will not tolerate rebellion." Gandhi responded with magnanimous good humor, "Your Majesty, you are a constitutional monarch, and may be pleased to leave it to your ministers."

On 1st November, 1931 Prime Minister Ramsay MacDonald, who was under a heavy political pressure from the imperialist lobby, declared at the close of the Round Table Conference that they had come to parting of ways and the ways would take different ways.

Gandhiji left the Conference with the following messages:

> "I do not know in what direction my path would be, but it does not matter to me. Even though I may have to go in an exactly opposite direction, you are still entitled to vote of thanks from the bottom of my heart."

On their return from England, Willingdon had Gandhiji and other leaders arrested. Jawaharlal Nehru's jail term also continued. The spontaneous civil disobedience movement which started after Gandhiji's arrest again proved to be a mass agitation. There were resumed firings by the police and the military forces. Press was gagged. Many members of the Central Assembly resigned.

Political situation was further complicated with the announcement of Communal Award in 1934, which resulted in Gandhiji's 21 days long protest fast. Gandhiji broke it after the Harijan leader Dr. B.R. Ambedkar came to an understanding with Gandhiji. As a result, a way out was found to keep the Harijan with the Hindu fold despite the mischievous Communal Award.

Meanwhile, Lord Willingdon in his policy of tyranny maneuvering communal riots, had set his sights deliberately on demolishing the fragile edifice of amity between his imperial country and subject India; thereby, he negated all Lord Irwin's earlier diplomacy.

Willingdon was acting under instructions from the Home Government. The latter was now much under the influence of pressure tactics of imperialist lobby headed by Churchill and Leo Amery. The authorities were now all out to crush the Congress, and stifle voices which did not orchestrate with official opinions. Aided by power of patronage and resources, the authorities were now openly pampering yes-men. These policies had admirantly succeeded in dividing the nationalist forces and had sown seeds of discord between majority Hindu community and the Muslims. In later years, this allowed the British to partition India in 1947.

Gandhiji resigned the formal membership of the Congress in 1934. In this context, he wrote to Sardal Patel (later Home Minister in Independent India) "I miss at this juncture the association and advice of Jawaharlal who is bound to be the rightful helmsman of the organisation in the near future." As planned by Gandhiji, Nehru eventually emerged as his political successor, though they differed on policy issues in some respects.

CIVIL DISOBEDIENCE—1932

Repression was at its peak. Representatives of Provinces gathered at Bombay to acquaint Gandhiji of woes of their respective provinces. Ordinances in N.W.F.P. and U.P. were promulgated which were described as New Year's gift. Gandhiji made a last minute appeal to the Viceroy to give relief to the peasantry. As no relief was forthcoming U.P. Congress advised the peasants to withhold the payment of rent and revenue temporarily pending negotiation. Pt. Jawaharlal Nehru, T.A. Sherwani and Purushottam Dass Tandon were arrested when going to Bombay to meet Mahatmaji. Government led by Viceroy Lord Willingdon let loose the whole machinery of the Government to strangle Congress. Mahatmaji and Sardar Patel were arrested on 4th January, 1932. All other leaders, who were still out were put behind bars. Congress was declared unlawful. Congress took this challenge bravely though this movement was faced on it un-awares. But, the Freedom Movement was conducted by the Congress in a magnificent manner. Lathi charges, firing, brutal assault, fines were the everyday feature.

Inspite of all these and other precautions taken by the Government, the annual session of the Congress was held at Delhi in 1932 and at Calcutta in 1933.

FORTY-SIXTH SESSION—1932 AT DELHI

Almost all India and Provincial leaders were in jail, yet, those free decided to hold the annual session at Delhi. Mahamana Pt. Madan Mohan Malviya was the President elect. Government took all possible steps not to allow the session. Notices were served to the management of all Dharamshalas and Hotels not to allow Congress delegates to stay. Tickets for Delhi from neighboring provinces were not issued. Inspite of all these precautions many hundred delegates reached Delhi. Pandit Madan Mohan Malviya President elect was arrested at Ghaziabad.

More than 500 delegates reached the venue of the session at Clock Tower, Chandni Chowk, Delhi. Seth Ranchod Das Amrit Lal of Ahmedabad presided with the adoption of following resolutions:

1. Reiterating complete Independence as the goal of Congress.
2. Whole hearted endorsing the revival of Civil Disobedience Movement.
3. Congratulating the nation on its splendid response to Mahatma Gandhiji's call.
4. Re-affirming deep faith in the non-violence and congratulating the country particularly to brave Pathans of N.W.F.P. upon their remaining non-violent in the face of the gravest provocation.

Several hundred delegates were arrested on that day. Many were injured in the lathi charge, but valiant Congressmen kept the Congress Flag flying.

FORTY-SEVENTH SESSION—1933 AT CALCUTTA

All the important Congressmen were in jail, Pandit Madan Mohan Malviya was to preside, but he had been arrested with Pt. Jawaharlal Nehru, Mrs. Vijay Laxmi Pandit, Dr. Syed Mahmood and Mr. S. Aney. Mrs. Nellini Sen Gupta was, therefore, called upon to preside. All resolutions of Delhi Congress of 1932 and Karachi Congress resolution on Fundamental Rights were reiterated.

FORTY-EIGHTH SESSION—1934 AT BOMBAY

DR. RAJENDRA PARSAD

This session was presided over by Dr. Rajendra Parsad. Civil Disobedience Movement of 1932 was suspended and ban on the Congress was withdrawn. Attendance was a record one. Some of the extracts from his presidential speech are:

- "Let us start with a clear slate on the work in front of us. The need of the hour is not for a bigger or more inspiring programme, but for the determination to achieve what little we may set before ourselves. The task is immense."
- "Our method is crystal clear. It is active, dynamic, non-violent mass action. We may fail once, we may fail twice but bound to succeed some day."

New Constitution of the Congress was adopted, whereby no one could become an office bearer of the Congress at any level, unless he was a habitual wearer of hand spun and hand woven Khadi. In this session the official Congress flag was adopted.

18

KAMLA NEHRU—A MARTYR TO DUTY

Despite oppressive measures of Lord Willingdon, Jawaharlal Nehru had spared nothing in organising the Congress. Under his immediate guidance, Congress workers in Bihar, Uttar Pradesh and even in Bengal were mobilised to carry on campaigns, sometime making issues of inequities in government and industrial establishments, but more often in the form of Kisan agitation. Nehru, Shibban Lal Saksena and Mohan Lal Saksena were most active in U.P. In Bihar, Swami Sahjanand Saraswati and in the south Prof. Ranga were most enthusiastic in agrarian agitations. Gujarat and Maharashtra were also astir.

In U.P., the ebullient Pandit Jawaharlal Nehru, despite best measures of the government, had succeeded, with other Congress workers in celebrating the Independence Proclamation Day on 26th January, 1934. When Jawaharlal Nehru returned to Allahabad from a hectic tour, he was arrested the very next day. He was sentenced to two years jail term on the charge of carrying an anti-government activities. First, he was kept in Alipur Jail, Calcutta. Later, however, he was brought to Naini Jail near Allahabad so that he could on occasion visit his ailing wife Kamla, who was gravely ill.

In jail he wrote his famous Autobiography, which he commenced writing in June, 1934. This was a master piece and is one of the most inspiring books which has been translated almost in all languages on a global scale. Imperial Britons were impressed by his literary calibre and his sacrifices.

In India, with other great public men and in England the labourites—among others even C.R. Attlee and George

Lansbury demanded vociferously Jawaharlal's release, especially as Nehru's wife was ill. In August, 1934 Nehru was allowed to spend a few days at his residence to see his wife. As she was suffering from tuberculosis, the doctors advised that she might be treated in Europe. Nehru took her there. But she pressed him to return to India, as he had been elected Congress President for the ensuing session at Lucknow. Kamla always preferred to abide by public duty rather than her own personal safety. Her condition became critical and she died on 28th February, 1936.

There was a national outpouring on the death of Smt. Kamla Nehru, who died after prolonged illness in Switzerland.

Nehru recollected his personal grief and plunged himself furiously in the work of reorganising the Congress cadres, apart from attending to such other public engagements which fell to his lot, as one who was a national hero of the highest stature. He dedicated his great work "My Story" the autobiography to Kamla "who is no more". Subsequently their heroic daughter Indira Gandhi, who rose to become in course of time a great Prime Minister of India, was equally conspicuous in displaying rare courage in crisis. She courted death in the cause of the integrity of the country by bullets of assassins in the circumstances which are well known, but too tragic to recount.

19

FORTY-NINTH SESSION—1936 AT LUCKNOW

This session was presided over by Pt. Jawaharlal Nehru. In his address he said:

- "We cannot isolate the Indian problem from that of the rest of the world.
- "Inevitably we take our stand with the progressive forces of the world which are ranged against Fascism and Imperialism. We have not to deal with one imperialism in particular, the oldest and most far-reaching of the modern world and that is the final argument for Indian Independence and for the severance of our connection with the British Empire.
- "Socialism is the only key to the solution of the world's problems—socialism in the scientific and economic sense. It is a vital creed which I hold with all my head and heart."

It was resolved to call a convention of the elected members of the legislatures, and members of the All India Congress Committee to consider the steps to be taken in framing the constitution, augmenting the election manifesto, and put forth demand for a Constituent Assembly.

FIFTIETH SESSION—1937 AT FAIZPUR

This session was held at Faizpur on December 27th and 28th, in 1937 under the Presidentship of Pt. Jawaharlal Nehru. Some of the extracts from his address are:

- "The elections have many things to teach us but the most astounding fact is this, where we went to direct the masses we won overwhelmingly. Our partial lack of success in some provinces was clearly due to the Congress organisations being confined to the cities and having little contact with the peasantry. We must remedy these failings and speak more the language of the masses and fashion our policy to meet their needs. We must carry the Congress organisation to every village, and the Congress message to meet every mud hut. We talk of Swaraj and Independence but in human terms it means relief to the masses from their unbearable sorrow and misery."

In this session Congress rejected the Government of India Act, 1935, which was imposed against the declared will of the people of the country.

Congress also condemned the Government policy in N.W.F.P. and against the suppression of the civil liberties.

This Congress Session was first to be held in a rural area.

FIFTY-FIRST SESSION—1938 AT HARIPUR

This session was presided over by Shri Subhash Chandra Bose. In his presidential address he said:

- "It is well known truism that every empire is based on the policy of divide and rule. I doubt if any empire in the world has practiced this policy so skillfully, systematically and ruthlessly.
- "I have no doubt in my mind that our chief national problems relating to the eradication of poverty, illiteracy and disease and the scientific production and distribution can be tackled along socialistic lines.

SHRI SUBHASH CHANDRA BOSE

- "It is the common platform of all anti-imperialist organisations trying for Indian emancipation. Let us, therefore, rally the whole country under the banner of Indian National Congress. We are fighting not for the cause of India alone but of humanity as well."

After the assumption of office by Congress ministries there was crisis in U.P. and Bihar on the question of release of political prisoners. Congress ministers resigned on 16th February, 1938. Governor agreed that after examination of individual cases the decision of the minister would be accepted.

Yet, another aspect of this Session related to regulating the struggle of people resident in the princely states for their democratic rights. Congress leaders continued to give them all support for establishment of responsible administrations in these states. However, at the Haripur Session, the Congress desired to concentrate efforts of this great organisation more on the liberation of British India, leaving the states people free to demand responsible government in the states as well. It resolved accordingly that "Internal struggles of the people of the States must not be undertaken in the name of the Congress. For this purpose, independent organisations should be started and continued where they exist already within the States." Thereby, support to responsible government even in princely states continued as an objective of the Indian National Congress, but it desired direct participation of local political organisations working in the States to be actively associated in this movement and to the fullest obligation for the same. The Congress leaders, Jawaharlal Nehru being the foremost, continued to give fullest support to movements in the states for democratisation in their respective states. Action liaison existed between those movements and the Congress struggle for freedom of India.

In practice, policy of the Congress was to support the progressive elements in the princely states as well, while forward looking rulers in the princely states were tolerated, the Congress encouraged Praja Mandal leaders to demand democratic rights in their respective states. Thus the alliance of miscreant rulers—both Indian and foreign—greatly weakened. A national movement for a sovereign independent India finally emerged from the most active patricipants of the people of British India as well as those residing in the princely states.

20

CONGRESS IN OFFICE IN THE PROVINCES—1937–39

The Promulgation of Government of India Act, 1935 provided another opportunity to Congressmen to resume the freedom struggle in the provincial and central legislatures.

The Federal part of the Act, was however, not implemented due to reluctance of the next Viceroy, Lord Linlithgow who succeeded Lord Willingdon. The Viceroy actually snubbed Sir Ganga Singh, the Maharaja of Bikaner, who was eager to have the Federal Scheme enforced.

The elections held under the Government of India Act for the provincial legislature, except for Burma, Ceylon and Aden which by virtue of this Act were separated from India, brought the Congress to power by the mammoth majority in eight provinces including Assam, Bengal, Bihar, Bombay, C.P., N.W.F.P., Madras, Orissa and U.P. Only in Bengal, Punjab and Sind, it failed to get a working majority. These results clearly showed that the prolonged repression of Lord Willingdon had the contrary result. The Congress had captured hearts of the masses. The electoral results were out in February, 1937. Among other factors, the Congress success was also due to Sardar Patel's organising skill, Pandit Jawaharlal Nehru's whirlwind tours and Rafi Ahmed Kidwai's courageous and tactful handling of the election campaign. The All India Congress Committee met at Delhi in March, 1937, with a convention of Congress members of the provincial legislatures. Pandit Jawarharlal Nehru, the Congress President, administered the following oath to the Congress legislatures:

"I, a member of this All India Convention, pledge myself to the service of India and to work in the legislatures and outside for the independence of India and the ending of exploitation and the poverty of the people. I pledge myself to work under the discipline of the Congress for the furtherance of the Congress ideals and objectives to the end that India may be free and independent and her millions freed from the heavy burdens they suffer from."

The Congress was assured that the governors would not ordinarily use veto powers. The Viceroy, in fact made a statement: "It is only when the issue between a Governor and his ministers constitutes a serious disagreement that any question of severing their partnerships need arise." The Congress Committee met at Wardha on 7th July, 1937 and authorised formation of Congress ministries in the provinces where the Congress had majority in view of the Viceroy's specific assurance. On the whole, these ministers functioned most successfully till the World War II commenced on 3rd September, 1939. Viceroy, Lord Linlithgow, on his own accord declared India's entry into the war contrary to all democratic norms. On this issue, the Congress ministries resigned from the office. Another confrontation was forced on the Congress.

Linlithgow enlisted the support of the Muslim League as a counterpoise to the Congress by whipping up communal discord. The League acted as a faithful ally of the Imperial masters, when it passed a resolution in 1940 demanding a separate state for the Muslims, namely Pakistan. Mohammed Ali Jinnah, a Bombay lawyer who was known for his peacock vanity played a crucial role as British ally.

21

FIFTY-SECOND SESSION—1939 AT TRIPURI

This session was presided over by Shri Subhash Chandra Bose. Up to 1939, Congress President used to be elected by consensus and final advice of Mahatmaji used to prevail. This year Subhash Chandra Bose contested the election against the wishes of Gandhiji. He was elected defeating Shri Sitaramaya. It was followed by the resignation of 12 out of 15 members of the Working Committee. Gandhiji did not attend the session as he was on fast unto death on the Rajkot issue. Following is the extract from his Presidential address (which was read by his elder brother Shri Sarat Chandra Bose due to illness of Subhash Chandra Bose):

- "This year promises to be an abnormal or extraordinary one in many ways. The time has come for us to raise the issue of Swaraj and submit our national demand to the British Government in the form of an ultimatum and give a certain time-limit within which a reply is to be expected. If no reply is received within this period or if an unsatisfactory reply is received within this period we should resort to mass civil disobedience or Satyagraha."

A procession of 51 pairs of bullocks was arranged but it had to be taken without him as the President elect Shri Subhash Chandra Bose was too ill to stand the strain.

Subject Committee passed a resolution stating "for the better feeling in the Congress the President is to form the Committee according to the wishes of Mahatma Gandhi." Gandhiji did not tender any advice regarding the formation of the Committee and said, "You are free to choose your Committee."

Under these circumstances it was not possible for him to run the Congress. Subhash Chandra Bose resigned from the Presidentship. Dr Rajendra Prasad was elected President in his place.

FORWARD BLOC

In May, 1939 Forward Bloc was formed as leftist wing of the Congress. Shri Subhash Chandra Bose who was President of Bengal Provincial Congress Committee, was expelled from the party for three years for defying the directive of the Congress President not to hold protest meeting on 9th July against the resolutions of the Congress.

22

SUBHASH CHANDRA BOSE— THE MAN OF ACTION

HIS INCARCERATION AND ACTIVITIES ABROAD

Like Jawaharlal Nehru, Subhash Chandra Bose had talked not only of freedom, in his address at Congress Session and also in his speeches, he had also stressed the imperative need for planning the construction. Under the influence, a Planning Committee was set up in 1939. Earlier he had given a plan of action for the Congress Party outside office, within the legislatures as well in the functioning of the government run by the Congress. He had formed the Forward Bloc to put pressure on the Congress leadership to mobilise actions on a massive scale to dislodge the British rulers from the Indian soil. Thereby, he was supplementing the freedom movement in his own way.

The British authorities had Bose arrested on 2nd July, 1940, as he was proving too aggressive. His popularity and views might hamper the war effort. Bose went on a hunger strike on 26th November, 1940. He was released on 5th December, 1940 only to be detained at his Elgin road residence in Calcutta. However, on 16/17 January, 1941, Bose made a dramatic dash to liberty which thrilled the whole country. He left his house by car. At Gamoh, he boarded a train, reached Peshawar without being detected by the British intelligence and crossed the border into Afghanistan on foot, disguised as a Pathan under the assumed name of Ziauddin. From Kabul, Bose travelled to Russia as an Italian. Then, he flew from

Moscow to Berlin. He met Hitler, but was disappointed by Hitler's attitude on the question of India's freedom.

THE INDIAN NATIONAL ARMY

When Japan entered the War, Shri Subhash Chandra Bose, at the invitation of the veteran revolutionary Rash Behari Ghosh, then resident in Japan, reached Malaya in a German

I.N.A.

U-Boat upto Madagaskar and thence in a Japanese sub-marine, he continued his marathon voyage on the high seas. He arrived in Tokyo, met Tojo and persuaded him to issue a declaration promising full independence to India if the Japanese win the war. He reached Singapore to assume leadership of the Indian National Army, which he organised from the recruits of Indian residents in East Asia and from amongst Indian prisoners of War, whom he persuaded to join his army.

The I.N.A. under Bose became a formidable force. It fought in Burma, captured part of the Indian territories and at Imphal fought against the British forces, which lay in the South East Asia Command of Lord Mountbatten.

After collapse of Japan, it is stated that he boarded a Japanese aircraft and left for Tokyo on 18th August, 1945. Enroute the plane was to land in Farmosa, where it was involved in a crash, in which Bose is stated to have died. However, the veracity of what actually happened to Bose remains a question mark of history, which he had so brilliantly illumined.

The formation of Indian National Army itself was a development of historic dimension. The British now knew that they could no longer depend on the mute loyalty of Indians, who had become impatient of the British rule. If the British did not transfer power to India, after a few years, in the word of Lord Wavell, the British might not be left with any power to transfer. Subhash, whatever his differences on the means to drive the British out of India, had been greatly influenced and moulded into a great nationalist due to his preliminary training as a Congressman.

A MEMORABLE EPISODE—REMOVAL OF UNION JACK FROM CENTRAL ASSEMBLY, 1940

Relations between the Congress leaders and the British Administration continued to be under grave stress in 1940. A significant episode occurred. This relates to the removal of Union Jack, from the Central Assembly Hall, as the British flag reminded Indians of their status of a subject people. Prof. N.G. Ranga, the veteran freedom fighter and now a Congress member of the Lok Sabha has recorded this memorable event in the following words:

> "One of the interesting things fraught with great future significance, that I was fortunate to do was to be one of a group of three (the other two

members being S.K.D. Paliwal and Mohan Lal Saksena) to climb to the top of the Assembly Hall and remove the Union Jack as a protest against its flying over the Chamber of elected members. The speaker was powerless, so was the government, to do anything against us, because neither by the rules nor by any specific resolution did the Assembly ever authorise the hoisting of the alien flag over its own Chamber. Gandhiji was requested by the Viceroy to persuade us to regret our action. We strongly refused to repent our action. Thus, did we herald about eight years in advance what was to happen in an official manner in 1947."

This showed the grim courage that the characteristic of Congressmen in that era of national struggle.

23

THE SECOND WORLD WAR AND THE CONGRESS

FIFTY-THIRD SESSION—1940 AT RAMGARH

MAULANA ABUL KALAM AZAD

This session was presided over by Maûlana Abul Kalam Azad. He said in his address:

- "It is equally inevitable that our decisions and conditions prevailing in India should affect the whole world. It was this consciousness and belief which brought about our decisions. We declared by these resolutions against reactionary movements like Fascism and Nazism which were directed against democracy and individual and national freedom. These movements were gaining strength day-by-day and India regarded them as the greatest danger to the world progress and peace. India's head and heart were with those people who were standing up for democracy and freedom and resisting the wave of reaction. It is impossible for us to forget the older danger which has proved unfortunately to be more fatal to the peace and freedom of nation than this new danger and which has in fact supplied the basis for this reaction. I refer to British Imperialism ! We are not distant spectators of this Imperialism as we are of the new reactionary movements."

- "India cannot endure the prospect of Nazism and Fascism but she is even more tired of British Imperialism. If India remains deprived of her national right of freedom, this would clearly mean that British Imperialism continued to flourish with all its traditional characteristics. Under such conditions India would, on no account, be prepared to lend a helping hand for the triumph of British Imperialism."

- "British Imperialism stands in the way of peace and justice today exactly as it did before the war. The Indian demand was a touchstone of Britains claim of fighting this war for peace and justice. They have been tested and found counterfeit and untrue."

Resolution regarding War and India's demand for the responsible Government immediately to enable India to play its role as an equal partner was adopted. One para of that resolution states:

- "The Congress hereby declares again that nothing short of Complete Independence can be accepted by the people of India. Indian freedom cannot exist within the orbit of Imperialism and Dominion Status or any other status within the imperial structure is wholly inapplicable to India, is not in keeping with the dignity of a great nation and would bind India in many ways to British policies and economic structure. The people of India alone can properly shape their own constitution and determine their relations with other countries of the world, through a Constituent Assembly elected on the basis of adult suffrage."

Many amendments to the resolutions were tabled, but were rejected. Gandhiji said while speaking on the resolution, "You cannot make me your General on your terms. Know, therefore, that I will insist on my conditions which are inexorable. You must understand that you have dealt with a dangerous man who may land you in an unexpected situation. Compromise is part and parcel of my nature. I will go to the Viceroy fifty times if I like it."

After this session there were many attempts with the British Government to accept the demand of Congress, to enable it to help the war efforts, with no response. In September, 1940 Congress Working Committee asked the British Government to give immediate effect in India, to its professions about democracy to the largest possible extent in order to convince the people of the sincerity of their declaration. Viceroy issued a statement on 18th October, 1940 to which Gandhiji reacted:

- "The Congress asked for bread and it got a stone."

Congress ministries in the provinces resigned. In August, 1940 Viceroy made offer of expanding the Viceroy's Council by appointing more Indians and also formation of War Advisory Committee. Congress Working Committee reacted adversely and Gandhiji issued following statement:

- "The Viceroy's pronouncement is deeply distressing. It widens the gulf between India as represented by the Congress and England. Thinking India, outside the Congress, has not welcomed the pronouncement. It does not dispel suspicion, neither does the pronouncement take note of the smouldering the discontentments. My own fear is that democracy is being wrecked. Britain cannot claim to stand for justice, if she fails to be just to India. India's disease is too deep to yield to any make-believe or half-hearted measures."

Pt. Nehru said, "The Congress must fight on. We cannot compromise with Imperialism."

Shri Rajagopalacharya made a sporting offer in answer to Mr. Amery's statement in House of Commons regarding minorities. He said, "Let Muslim League be invited to nominate Prime Minister and let him form a national Government."

INDIVIDUAL SATYAGRAHA

After all these efforts, individual Satyagraha was started on 17th October, 1940, in most restricted character to avoid embarrassment to the Government in its hour of trial. Shri Vinoba Bhave, first Satyagrahi, nominated by Gandhiji, was arrested. Pt. Jawaharlal Nehru was to follow him, but he was arrested on 31st October, 1940 and was sentenced to four years' imprisonment. Every Satyagrahi was to get the permission of Gandhiji. Before offering Satyagraha he was to inform the authorities his intention to offer satyagraha and day and time.

The campaign went on smoothly for 14 months. Viceroy meanwhile expanded its council with non-official majority, which was a mockery. Mr. Amery, Secretary of State of India in his statement on 1st August, in the House of Commons emphatically ruled out any transfer of power and said sarcastically "India is not a country as there is Belgium or Holland and in any respect India is much more like Europe than it was like an individual country." This patted the separationists on the back.

On August 15, 1941, Prime Minister Churchill and President Roosevelt made an eight point declaration known as Altlantic Charter. The people of European countries saw their liberty and salvation whereas people of Asia and Africa read in it their perpetual slavery—Churchill did not think that Charter to be applicable to India though Mr. Attlee, Deputy Prime Minister at that time stated 'The declaration will be equally applicable to all races.' When Gandhiji was asked to express his opinion said that "his silence was more elequent."

The war was approaching at the gate of India. Singapore, Rangoon had fallen at the hands of Japan. British government sent Sir Stafford Cripps, with certain proposals which was nothing more than Balkanisation of India.

Meanwhile Subhash Chandra Bose had left India and it was ripe in all quarters that Japanese Army under the Command of Subhash Chandra Bose was going to liberate India. In an article in Harijan, Gandhiji wrote:

- "I have no desire to exchange British for any other rule. I want to resist with all my might the charge of inviting Japan to India. I want India to oppose Japan to a Man."

- "I am more interested than the British in keeping Japan away, for British defeat in Indian Waters may mean only the loss of India, but if Japan wins, India looses every thing."

In an article on 19th April, 1942 published in Harijan Mahatmaji gave public impression to the theory, which was crystalized into Quit India Movement. Mahatmaji worte "The presence of British in India is an invitation to Japan to invade India. The withdrawl removes the bait."

In other article Gandhiji wrote:

- "In this struggle every risk has to be run in order to cure ourselves the biggest disease—a disease which has slapped our manhood and almost made us feel as if we must be for ever slaves. It is an unsufferable thing. The cost of a cure I know will be heavy. No price is too heavy to pay for the deliverance."

QUIT INDIA MOVEMENT

After the failure of Cripps Mission Congress Working Committee met on 14th July, 1942 at Wardha and adopted 1700 words resolution demanding withdrawal of British from India, the concluding para is:

- "In making the proposal for the withdrawal of British rule the Congress has no desire whatsoever to embarrass Great Britain and Allied power in the prosecution of war. The Congress is therefore agreeable to the stationing of armed forces of Allies in India, should they so desire, in order to ward and resist the Japanese aggression and to protect and help China."
- "The Congress will be reluctantly compelled to utilise all the non-violent strength it might have gathered since 1920 when it adopted non-violence as a part of its policy, for vindication of political right and liberty."

When asked, as to whether the Congress was prepared to negotiate, Gandhiji said "There is no room for negotiation, Either they recognise Independence or they don't." Maulana Azad said "It refers to India's right of Independence. It is certianinly not a matter for negotiation."

In order to avoid conflict Gandhiji wrote in Harijan dated 2nd August, 1942 under the Caption "A Plea for Reason" presenting the Congress case.

Gandhiji also wrote to American friends:

- "I assert that I would not have asked my country to invite Great Britain to withdraw her rule from India, if I had not seen at once that for the sake of great Britain and Allied cause, it was necessary for Britain boldly to perform the duty of freeing India from bondage. By that supreme act of justice Britain would have taken away all causes for seething his content of India.
- "You will do a grevious wrong to the Allied cause if you do not shift the truth from the chaff while there is yet time. Just to think of it. Is there anything wrong in the Congress demanding the constitutional recognition of India's Independence."

All such sincere efforts of Mahatma Gandhi failed, All India Congress Committee met at Bombay on 7th August, 1942 to consider menace of Japanese aggression and to adopt a resolution known as QUIT INDIA RESOLUTION (Appendix V)—Congress President Maulana Azad in his opening remarks said:

- "The menace of aggression to India was ever increasing and danger which was only a distant one months ago, was approaching. The Congress wanted to see that every Indian took part in resisting aggression."
- "The Quit India's demand does not mean the physical removal of all Britishers from India, but it means transfer of charge."

After Maulana Azad Gandhiji in his address said, "This is a crucial hour. If we keep quiet and do not play our part it will not be right on our part."

Pt. Jawaharlal Nehru while moving the resolution said:

- "The resolution was in no sense a challenge to any one. If the British Government accepted the proposal it would change the whole position for the better for both internal and international from every point of view."

Sardar Patel, seconding the resolution said:

- "If America and England were still thinking that they could fight enemies from India without the cooperation of 400 millions people they were foolish. It must dawn on the people that this war was a people's war and they should

QUIT INDIA MOVEMENT

fight for their country and for their freedom." He also warned that "Fight before us is going to be tough one."

After the adoption of Quit India resolution Gandhiji made one of the longest speeches (2 hours) with solemn and stern warning said:

- "I shall strain every move for peace. Let there be final peace among countries. I will not be afraid to stand against the whole world for God is with us. I shall wage my lonely battle even if whole of India forsake me. Congress has committed no crime by demanding complete Independence for the country. I have pledged my support to Congress and Congress will Do or Die."

AICC concluded its session at 10 p.m. on 8th August. By morning of 9th August, Gandhiji and members of Congress Working Committee and all other important Congressmen, Provincial leaders, Office bearers were arrested and those escaped went underground. Gandhiji, Kasturba and his faithful secretaries Mahadev Desai and Shri Peary Lal were taken to Agha Palace at Poona and members of working committee to Ahmedgarh Fort.

There was stir, anger and resentment in the country. Mass agitation started spontaneously against midnight arrest. Telephone wires were cut, poles were uprooted, railway lines were disrupted, Government buildings were set on fire. Thousands students left colleges and Universities. Members of Governor General council were picketed. Universities were occupied by the Military. Even sober leader Pt. Madan Mohan Malviya, Vice Chancellor of Banaras University who founded the University with great efforts said, "Let the University be destroyed and bombed. If India live thousand universities will emerge."

To suppress the agitation the Military was called in big cities and towns on 533 occasions. There was no government in most of the areas in Bihar and Maharashtra and at various other places. In some places parallel governments were established. In most parts of the country presence of government was not felt. Planes were used to bombard villages. Govenment distributed a booklet under the caption Congress Responisbility for Disturbances. Gandhiji from his detention wrote to Viceroy "The movement was not started by the resolution of 8th August. Before I could function they arrested, not only who was to lead and guide the movement if negotiation failed, but principle Congressmen all over India. Thus it was not I, but the Government who started the movement."

Mr. Amery in the House of commons denied the use of aeroplanes to bombard.

According to Govern-ment's statement in the Central Assembly upto November, 1942:

Persons arrested	60,229
Persons detained under D.I.R.	18,000
Persons killed by police or military firing	940
Persons injured	1630

According to non-official statement 7000 is the number of dead. In Central Provinces, women were raped by the police officials in village Chimur in Chanda District. Prof. Bhansali undertook fast at the residence of Shri Aney (member of Viceroy's Executive Council). He was arrested and lodged in Delhi jail. He was released and rearrested. After 36 days' fast, a settlement was arrived with C.P. Government on 12th January, 1943.

Rigid press censorship was imposed. In protest against these restrictions most of the news papers suspended their publications for one day. Speeches of members of the British Government, Viceroy, Governors and New Year Honours list were not published.

Mr. William Phillips personal representative of President Roosevelt was not allowed to see Mahatmaji though he specially came to know the real position.

Khan Bahadur Allah Bux Premier of Sind renounced his title in protest against the repressive policy of the Government and on his refusal to resign, he was dismissed.

Dr. Shyama Parshad Mukherjee Finance Minister in Bengal resigned his office on 16th November, 1942.

In nutshell Government ruthlessly adopted all the possible repressive measures to suppress and crush the movement. What else could be expected when Home Member declared Congress as an internal enemy.

Gandhiji during his internment in Agha Khan Palace lost Kasturba—mother of millions and his faithful Secretary Shri

Mahadev Desai. Gandhiji also went on fast unto death in Agha Khan Palace. Government even made arrangement for his last rites in jail thinking that he would not survive.

Country faced an unparalleled and man-made famine in Bengal. Four million people died due to hunger and epidemic.

RECALL OF LINLITHGOW

Lord Linlithgow was recalled on 20th October, 1943 after having served as the Viceroy for seven and a half years. His successor, Field Marshall Lord Wavell who was a brilliant top war lord of Britain, had many failures in the Far East and later in Africa in the Second World War. Churchill never liked him. C.R Attlee also did not fully trust Wavell for his diplomatic calibre. Churchill, who had an ugly note of racism in his character did not like Wavell to succeed as the Viceroy. He was not favourably impressed, when Wavell tried to contain the rigour of the Bengal famine. Wavell's plea for shipping facilities to import wheat from Australia to feed the hungry people of Bengal was rejected by the Home Government. His attempts to conciliate the Indian public opinion in Simla Conference and subsequent negotiations failed partly as the parameters of Wavell's authority to negotiate was not clearly defined by his Home Government. Further, his proposals were also wrecked due to intransigence of Mohammed Ali Jinnah.

Another tragic element which dominated Wavell's character related to his faulty opinions about Mahatma Gandhi and Jawaharlal Nehru. In his diary published as the "Viceroy's Journal" edited by Penderell Moon, in Wavell's estimation the Mahatma was a suspect. Even so, Gandhi was released. Wavell requested his Home Government that he "might be allowed to talk politics" with Indian leaders. Wavell was prevented from doing so by the Secretary of State.[1] Wavell later told King George VI that "put up against Gandhi he was as a rabbit faced by stoat."

The most costly mistake which Wavell made was to pamper the Muslim League, which he placed at par with the Indian National Congress.

---

[1] Lewin, Renald; *The Chief Field Marshall Lord Wavell, Commander-in-Chief and The Viceroy*—1939 –1947, Hutchinson, London, 1980, p. 220.

24

FINAL TRIUMPH

Gandhiji was released unconditionally on medical grounds in 1944. He, after recouping health, took an initiative to enable the Congress Working Committee to withdraw movement. He sought an interview with the Viceroy which was refused. With a view to end deadlock, he even took an initiative to have a dialogue with Mr. M.A. Jinnah.

In 1945 other leaders also came out of jail. The war ended. Labour Government under Mr. Attlee came into power. Attlee declared that British Government is determined to hand over power to Indians latest by June, 1948. Elections to Provincial Assemblies were held. Cabinet Mission visited India under Secretary of State for India, Lord Pethick Lawrence in 1946. Cabinet Committee's proposals were not acceptable either to Congress or Muslim League. The Muslim League was determined to get India partitioned. Muslims started communal riots in Punjab and Bengal which had its reactions in Hindu majority provinces. Thousands lost lives. These developments forced Congress to think about partition though the same was opposed with all force at their disposal, by Gandhiji and Abdul Ghaffar Khan.

Mr. C.R. Attlee Prime Minister of England announced at the time of departure of the Cabinet Committee:

- "My colleagues are going to India with the intention of using their utmost endeavours to help her to attain her freedom as speedily and fully as possible. What form of Government is to replace the present one is for India to decide, but our desire is to help her to set up forth with the machinery for making the decision."

FIFTY-FOURTH SESSION—1946 AT MEERUT

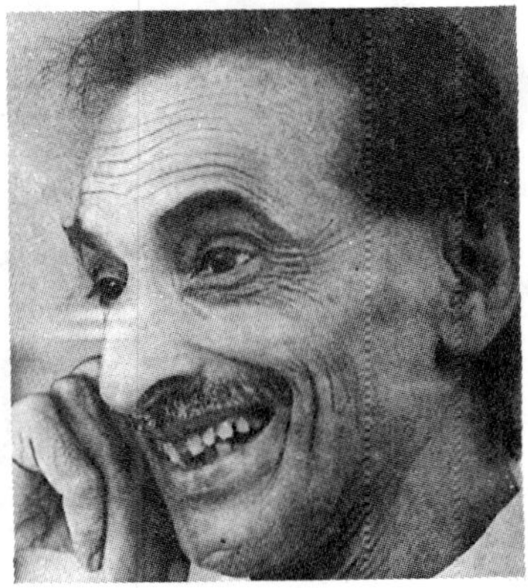

ACHARYA KRIPLANI

This session was presided over by Acharya Kriplani a veteran Congressman who joined Gandhiji on his return from South Africa in 1916, as Gandhiji's close colleague in Champeron Satyagrah. He was member of the Congress Working Committee and its General Secretary for a number of years. He was also considered master of Gandhian ideology and written several books.

This session which was held after six years was decided to be organised on a big scale as a Diamond Jubilee Session but owing to the breakout of communal riots, only a small session confined to delegates and few visitors was actually held. Subjects Committee Pandal was used for open session. Representatives from Overseas Indians from various countries attended the session. Presence of I.N.A. heroes General Shah Nawaz and others and I.N.A. orchestra under captain Ram Singh created a new life. Due to curfew in the city, Congress Session tickets were considered as curfew pass by the authorities.

Condolence resolution was adopted in memory of those who expired during last six years such as Mahamana Pt. Madan Mohan Malviya, Rabindra Nath Tagore, Jamna Lal Bajaj, Bhula Bhai Desai, Kasturba Gandhi, Mahadev Desai etc. A resolution reviewed the happenings of the last six years and homage was paid to those who died and suffered in the cause of the country's freedom. It also expressed alarm at the use of atom bomb as a war weapon. It also ratified decision of the Congress to join a Constituent Assembly.

During Acharya Kriplani's Presidentship several efforts were made to have some understanding with the Muslim League to avoid partition of the country. A cabinet mission with several proposals visited India. After the failure of the cabinet mission and deteriorating communal situation, Lord

Wavell was recalled and Lord Mountbatten took over as Governor General of India. Seeing further deterioration of communal situation and destruction of lives and properties of the minority community throughout the country, date of Transfer of Power which was earlier fixed for June 1948 was advanced to 15th August, 1947. British Parliament adopted Indian Independence Act 1947 on 1st July, 1947 creating two Dominions namely Pakistan and Bharat i.e. India, giving freedom to join 600 odd Indian states to any of the Dominions. This stage for Transfer of Power and Partition of the country was set under the Presidentship of Acharyaji with deep regret to him, Mahatmaji and others.

NOTE

Acharyaji resigned from Presidentship in November 1947 due to his differences with the Government. Acharyaji writes in his book, 'Gandhi, His Life and Mission' that his candidature for the presidentship of Meerut session was strongly opposed by Pt. Jawaharlal Nehru, Maulana Abul Kalam Azad, and others and tried to persuade Gandhiji not to give his consent on Acharyaji's candidature. These very leaders who opposed Acharyaji's candidature in Meerut session supported his candidature in 1950 against the candidature of Shri Purushottam Das Tandon.

THE DAWN OF FREEDOM

Bright luminous Dawn ! rose-red, radiant rejoicing !
Showing the traveller his road; the cattle their pasture new;
Rouse the beasts of the Earth to their truthful myriad voicing,
Leader of lightful days ! softening the soil with dew.
Wide-expanded Dawn ! Open the gates of the morning;
Waken the singing birds ! Guide thou the truthful light
To uttermost shade of the shadow, for, see you ! the dawning
Is born, white-shining, out of the gloom of the night.

(*Rigveda*)

"O lovely dawn of freedom that breaks in gold and purple over the ancient capital of 'Prithviraj', O splendid flag of new born India to be unfurled on the morrow over the Red Fort of Shahjehan. We pay you the homage of our dedicated heart and hands and pledge ourselves to translate into glorious deeds the dreams that were our share and inspiration in the long darkness of our bondage."

Sarojini Naidu
August 14–15, 1947

The suffering and the sacrifices of countless men and women finally bore fruit and India woke up to freedom on the midnight of August 14-15. The travails and tribulations had come to an end. The joyous moment of having broken off the shackles of subjugation was there inspite of the pain and agony of Partition. The time had come when we could look forward to the sun of freedom and the opportunity that freedom brings.

The ceremony of the Assumption of Power by India through her chosen representatives in the Constituent Assembly which had begun its Constitution-making activity on December 9, 1946, was fixed to take place on the midnight of August 14–15. The time chosen was perhaps to commemorate another midnight session, equally memorable, when a similar hazardous journey was undertaken and equally solemn dedication made. Some of the very men and women who took part in the drama on August 14–15—and many others who thronged and cheered on the road outside and lit lamps and put up flags and festoons in towns and villages, had taken part in that earlier session and in the struggle that began on that midnight of December 31, 1929–Jan. 1, 1930 in Lahore.

And yet how different was the setting. The city of thatch and canvass on the banks of the Ravi, the biting winternight and this gilded chamber, air-conditioned, lit by chandelier lights, the decorous benches and galleries. What a tame picture they make when we recall the tumultuous scenes, the midnight revelry led by the Rashtrapati himself, from camp to camp on that earlier midnight. It was strange that a revolution had culminated in this way and an event of such colossal historical importance as the freedom of 400 million people was recorded in this brief manner.

The session in the chamber began at 10-45 p.m. The galleries were full of a colourful crowd. A surging mass had gathered outside. The proceeding commenced with the 'Vande Mataram' sung by Mrs. Sucheta Kripalani, the wife of the then Congress President. This was followed by a brief opening address by the President of the Consembly, Dr. Rajendra Parsad. Pandit Nehru then moved the pledge. He made a stirring speech with deep emotion. The motion was seconded by Choudhury Khaliquzzaman and supported by

Dr. S. Radhakrishnan. The members of the Constituent Assembly took the pledge of dedicating themselves "to the service of India and her people to the end so that this ancient land attain her rightful and honoured place in the world and make her full and willing contribution to the promotion of world peace and welfare of mankind."

The pledge was read out by Dr. Rajendra Parsad first in Hindi and then in English and repeated sentence by sentence by members rising in their seats, followed by blowing of conch-shells and lusty shouts of "Mahatma Gandhi Ki Jai".

Before Pandit Nehru moved the pledge; a two minute silence was observed in memory of those who died in the struggle for freedom in India and elsewhere.

Both Dr. Parsad and Pandit Nehru paid striking tributes to Mahatma Gandhi's outstanding contributions to the cause of India's freedom. Mention of Gandhiji's name practically sent the House into hysterics.

JOY LIT UP GANDHIJI'S FACE

The only place that celebrated the 15th of August with a sincerely felt joy and abandonment was Calcutta where Gandhiji had decided to pass the historic night. What actually transpired on that night and the glorious dawn of the 15th August was something like a miracle. As if by magic the year long tension and animosity had disappeared and a mighty, emotional upsurge of Hindu-Muslim fraternisation swept the city from end to end. It was a touching scene to witness.

When the news was conveyed to Gandhiji, a smile of joy lit up his face. His deep anguish at the suffering of the people, Hindus and Muslims, on the dusty Punjab roads, and in improvised shelters, must have been forgotten for this moment, Gandhiji celebrated the 15th of August, in Calcutta by fasting and praying in which Mr. Suhrawardy kept him company.

Dr. Rajendra Parsad moved the following resolution from the Chair admist thunderous cheers and acclamation:

- "I propose that it will be intimated to His Excellency the Viceroy that Constituent Assembly of India has assumed the power for the Government of India, and the Constituent Assembly of India has endorsed the recommendation that Lord Mountbatten be the Governor-General of India from August 15, 1947, and that this message be conveyed forthwith to Lord Mountbatten by the President and Pandit Nehru."

The House approved it admist acclamation. Mrs. Hansa Mehta then presented the National Flag of India to the Indian Constituent Assembly. In presenting the Flag to Dr. Rajendra Parsad, Mrs. Mehta said: "It is in the fitness of things that the first flag that is flying over this august House should be the gift from the women of India."

Dr. Parsad showed the Flag round. Proceedings came to a close with the singing of "Hindustan Hamara", a poem by Dr. Iqbal and "Janaganamana Adhinayaka" by Rabindranath. Mrs. Sucheta Kripalani conducted the chorus.

A TRYST WITH DESTINY

Moving the resolution prescibing an oath for the members in the Constituent Assembly, free India's first Prime Minister, Pandit Jawaharlal Nehru, declared:

Long years ago we made a tryst with destiny, and now the time comes when we shall redeem our pledge, not wholly or in full measure, but very substantially. At the stroke of the midnight hour, when the world sleeps, India will awake to life and freedom. A moment comes, which comes but rarely in history, when we step out from the old to the new, when an age ends, and when the soul of a nation, long suppressd, finds utterance. It is fitting that at this solemn moment we take the pledge of dedication to the service of India and her people and to the still larger cause of humanity.

At the dawn of history India started on her unending quest, and trackless centuries are filled with her striving and the grandeur of her success and her failures. Through good and ill fortune alike she has never lost sight of that quest or forgotton the ideals which gave her strength. We end today a period of ill fortune and India discovers herself again. The achievement we celebrate today is but a step, an opening of opportunity, to the greater triumphs and achievements that await us. Are we brave enough and wise enough to grasp this opportunity and accept the challenge of the future?

Freedom and power bring responsibility. That responsibility rests upon this Assembly, a sovereign body representing the sovereign people of India. Before the birth of freedom we have endured all the pains of labour and our hearts are heavy with the memory of this sorrow. Some of those pains continue even now. Nevertheless, the past is over and it is the future that beckons to us now.

That future is not one of ease or resting but of incessant striving so that we may fulfil the pledges we have so often taken and the one we shall take today. The service of India means the service of the millions who suffer. It means the ending of poverty and ignorance and disease and inequality of opportunity. The ambition of the greatest man of our generation has been to wipe every tear from every eye. That may be beyond us, but as long as there are tears and suffering, so long our work will not be over.

And so we have to labour and to work, and work hard, to give reality to our dreams. Those dreams are of India, but they are also for the world, for all the nations and peoples are too closely knit together today for any one of them to imagine that it can live apart. Peace has been said to be indivisible; so is freedom, so is prosperity now, and so also is disaster in this One World that can no longer be split into isolated fragments.

To the people of India, whose representatives we are, we make an appeal to join us with faith and confidence in this great adventure. This is no time for petty and destructive criticism, no time for ill-will or blaming others. We have to build the noble mansion of free India where all her children may dwell.

I beg to move, Sir,

That it be resolved that:

(1) After the last stroke of midnight, all members of the Constituent Assembly present on this occasion, do take the following pledge:

- 'At this solemn moment when the people of India, through suffering and sacrifice, have secured freedom, I, . . ., a member of the Constituent Assembly of India, do dedicate myself in all humility to the service of India and her people to the end that this ancient land attain her rightful place in the world and make her full and willing contribution to the promotion of world peace and the welfare of mankind;'

(2) Members who are not present on this occasion do take the pledge (with such verbal changes as the President may prescribe) at the time they next attend a session of the Assembly.

Dr. Rajendra Parsad delivered a memorable speech on the morning of the 15th. He said:

- "Let us in this momentous hour of our history, when we are assuming power for the governance of our country, recall in grateful remembrance the services and sacrifices of all those who laboured and suffered for the achievement of the independence we are attaining today. Let us on this historic occasion pay our homage to the maker of our modern history, Mahatma Gandhi, who has inspired and guided us through all these years of trial and travail and who inspite of the weight of years is still working in his own way to complete what is left yet unaccomplished.

  "Let us gratefully acknowledge that while our achievement is in no small measure due to our own sufferings and sacrifice, it is also the result of world forces and events and last though not least it is the consummation and fulfilment of the historic traditions and democratic ideals of the British race whose farsighted leaders and statesmen saw the vision and gave the pledge which are being redeemed today. We are happy to have in our midst as a representative of that race Viscount Mountbatten of Burma and his consort who have worked hard and played such an important part in bringing this about during the closing scenes of this drama. The period of domination by Britain over India ends today and our relationship with Britain henceforward going to rest on a basis of equality, of mutual goodwill and mutual profit.

  "It is undoubtedly a day of rejoicing. But there is only one thought which mars and detracts from the fullness of this happy event. India, which was made by God and Nature to be one, which culture and tradition and history of millenniums have made one, is divided today and many there are on the other side of the boundary who would much rather be on this side. To them we send a word of cheer and assurance and ask them not to give way to panic of despair but to live with faith and courage in peace with their neighbours and fulfil the duties of loyal citizenship and thus win their rightful place. We send our greetings to the new Dominion which is being established today there and wish it the best luck in its great work of governing that region and making all its citizens happy and prosperous. We feel assured that they all will be treated fairly and justly without any distinction or discrimination. Let us hope and pray that the day will come when even those who have insisted upon and brought about this division will realise India's essential oneness and we shall be united once again. We must realise however that this can be brought about not by force but by largeheartedness and co-operation and by managing our affairs on this side as to attract those who have parted. It may appear to be a dream but it is no more fantastic a dream than that of those who wanted a division and may well be realised even sooner that we dare hope for today.

"More than a day of rejoicing it is a day of dedication for all of us to build the India of our dreams. Let us turn our eyes away from the past and fix our gaze on the future. We have no quarrel with other nations and countries and let us hope no one will pick a quarrel with us. By history and tradition we are a peaceful people and India wants to be at peace with the world. India's Empire outside her own broders had been of a different kind from all other Empires. India's conquests have been a conquest of spirit which did not impose heavy chains of slavery, whether of iron or of gold, on others but tied other lands and other peoples to her with the more enduring ties of golden silk—of culture and civilisation, of religion and knowledge (*gyan*). We shall follow that same tradition and shall have no ambition save that of contributing our little mite to the building of peace and freedom in a war-distracted world by holding aloft the banner under which we have marched to victory and placing in a practical manner in the hands of the world the great weapon of non-violence which has achieved this unique result. India has a great part to play. There is something in her life and culture which has enabled her to survive the onslaughts of time and today we witness a new birth full of promise, if only we prove ourselves true to our ideals.

"Let us resolve to create conditions in this country when every individual will be free and provided with the wherewithal to develop and rise to his fullest stature, when poverty and squalor and ignorance and ill-health will have been vanished, when the distinction between high and low, between rich and poor, will have disappeared, when religion will not only be professed and preached and practised freely but will have become a cementing force for binding man to man and not serve as a disturbing and disrupting force dividing and separating, when untouchability will have been forgotten like an unpleasant night dream, when exploitation of man by man will have ceased, when facilities and special arrangements will have been provided for the *addimjatis* of India and for all others who are backward, to enable them to catch up to others and when this land will have not only enough food to feed its teeming millions but will once again have become a land flowing with rivers of milk, when men and women will be laughing and working for all they are worth in fields and factories, when every cottage and hamlet will be humming with the sweet music of village handicrafts and maids will be busy with them and singing to their tune—when the sun and the moon will be shining on happy homes and loving faces.

"To bring all this about we need all the idealism and sacrifice, all the intelligence and diligence, all the determination and the power of organisation that we can muster. We have many parties and groups with differing ideals and ideologies. They are all trying to convert the country to their own ideologies and to mould the constitution and the administration to suit their own view point. While they have the right to do so the country and the nation have the right to demand loyalty from them. All must realise that what is needed most today is a great constructive effort—not strife, hard solid work—not argumentation and let us hope that all will be prepared to make their contribution. We want the peasant to grow more food, we want the workers to produce more goods, we want our industrialists to use their intelligence, tact and resourcefulness for the common good. To all we must assure conditions of decent and healthy life and opportunities for self-improvement and self-realisation.

"Not only have the people to dedicate themselves to this great task that lies ahead but those who have so far been playing the role of rulers and regulators of the lives of our men and women have to assume the role of servants. Our army has won undying glory in distant lands for its bravery and great fighting qualities. Our soldiers, sailors and airmen have to realise that they now form a national army on whom devolves the duty not only of defending the freedom which we have won but also to help in a constructive way in building up a new life. There is no place in the armed forces of our country which is not open to our people, and what is more they are required to take the highest places as soon as they can so that they may take full charge of our defences. Our public servants in various departments of Government have to shed their role as rulers and have to become true servants of the people that their compeers are in all free countries. The people and the Government on their side have to give them their trust and assure them conditions of service in keeping with the lives of the people in whose midst they have to live and serve.

"We welcome the Indian States which have acceded to India and to their people we offer our hands of comradeship. To the princes and the rulers of the States we say that we have no designs against them. We trust they will follow the example of the King of England and become constitutional rulers. They would do well to take as their model the British monarchical system which has stood the shock of two successive world wars when so many other monarchies in Europe have toppled down.

"To Indians settled abroad in British Colonies and elsewhere we send our good wishes and assurance of our abiding interest in their welfare. To our minorities we give the assurance that they will receive fair and just treatment and their rights will be respected and protected.

"One of the great tasks which we have in hand is to complete the constitution under which not only will freedom and liberty be assured to each and all but which will enable us to achieve and attain and enjoy its fulfilment and its fruits. We must accomplish this task as soon as possible so that we may begin to live and work under a constitution of our own making, of which we may all be proud, and which it may become our pride and privilege to defend and to preserve to the lasting good of our people and for the service of mankind. In framing that constitution we shall naturally draw upon the experience and knowledge of other countries and nations no less than on our own traditions and surroundings and may have at times to disregard the lines drawn by recent history and lay down new boundary lines not only of Provinces but also of distribution of powers and functions. Our ideal is to have a constitution that will enable the people's will be expressed and enforced and that will not only secure liberty to the individual but also reconcile and make it subservient to the common good.

"We have up to now been taking a pledge to achieve freedom and to undergo all sufferings and sacrifices for it. Time has come when we have to take a pledge of another kind. Let no one imagine that the time for work and sacrifice is gone and the time for enjoying the fruits thereof has come. Let us realise that the demand on our enthusiasm and capacity for unselfish work in the future will be as great as, if not greater than, what it has even been before. We have, therefore, to dedicate ourselves that we may have the strength, the wisdom and courage to fulfil it."

LORD MOUNTBATTEN'S ADDRESS

Lord Mountbatten in his address read a message of goodwill from His Majesty the King to the new dominion of India. Recounting the history of negotiations for Indian Freedom, Lord Mountbatten paid a homage to the practical capacity for compromise of the leaders of the country. He said that from August 15, 1947 he was there as the servant of the Indian people, having agreed to serve as the first Governor-General of free India on the invitation of the people's representatives.

Appendix I

CONGRESS OBJECTS*

The promotion of personal intimacy and friendship amongst all the more earnest workers in our country's cause in various parts of the Empire.

The eradication by direct friendly personal intercourse of all possible race, creed, or provincial prejudices amongst all lovers of our country and fuller development and consolidation of those sentiments of national unity that had their origin in their beloved Lord Ripon's ever memorable reign.

The authoritative record after this has been carefully elicited by the fullest discussion of the matured opinions of the educated classes in India on some of the more important and pressing of the social questions of the day.

The determination of the lines upon and methods by which during the next twelve months it is desirable for native politicians to labour in the public interests

* Extract from the Presidential Address to the first Indian National Congress held at Bombay, 1885.

Appendix II

LAHORE RESOLUTION AT MIDNIGHT OF 31ST DECEMBER, 1929 AND 1ST JANUARY, 1930

This Congress is of the opinion that nothing is to be gained in the existing circumstances by the Congress being represented at the proposed Round Table Conference. The Congress declared that Swaraj shall mean *Complete Independence*. It declared the entire scheme of Nehru Committee's Report to have lapsed and hopes that all Congressmen will henceforth devote their exclusive attention to the attainment of Complete Independence for India. The Congress calls upon Congressmen and others taking part in the national movement to abstain from participating directly or indirectly in future elections and directs the present Congress members of the Legistlatures and Committees to resign their seats. This Congress appeals to the nation to zealously persecute the constructive programme of the Congress and authorise the All India Congress Committee whenever it deems fit to launch upon a programme of Civil Disobedience movement including non payment of taxes whether in selected areas or otherwise and under such safeguard as it may consider necessary.

Vande Mataram

Sujlam Suflam, Malyaj Sheetlam
Shasyashyamlam Mataram

Shubhra Jyotsna Pulkit Yaminim
Phullakusumit Drumadalshobhinim,
Suhasinim Sumadhur Bhashinim
Sukhdam Vardam Mataram.

Saptkotikanth-kalkal-Ninad Karale
Dwisaptkotibhujrdhritkharkarwale,
Abla ken Ma Et Bale.

Bahubal Dharinim Namami Tarinim
Ripudal Varinim Mataram.

Tumi Vidya Tumi Dharmma,
Tumi Hridi Tumi Marmma,
Twam Hi Prana Shareere
Bahute Tumi Ma Shakti,
Hridye Tumi Ma Bhakti,
Tomarayi Pratima Gadi Mandire Mandire.

Twam Him Durga Dashpraharandharini
Kamla Kamal-Dal-Viharini
Vani Vidyadayini Namami Twam
Namami Kamlam Amlam Atulam

Sujlam Suflam Mataram,
Vande Mataram,
Shyamlam Sarlam Susmitam Bhushitam
Dharnim Bharnim Mataram.

वन्देमातरम्

सुजलां सुफलां मलयज् शीतलां
शस्यश्यामलां मातरम्।
शुभ्र-ज्योत्स्ना-पुलकित यामिनीं
फुल्लकुसुमित-द्रुमदलशोभिनीम्,

सुहासिनीं सुमधुर भाषिणीम्
सुखदां वरदां मातरम्।।

सप्तकोटिकंण्ठ-कलकल-निनाद कराले
द्विसप्तकोटिभुजैर्धृतखरकरवाले,
अबला केन मा एत बले।

बहुबलधारिणीं नमामि तारिणीम्
रिपुदल वारिणीं मातरं।।

तुमि विद्या तुमि धर्म्म, तुमि ह्रदि तुमि मर्म्म,
त्वं हि प्राणाः शरीरे।

बाहुते तुमि मा शक्ति, ह्रदये तुमि मा भक्ति,
तोमारइ प्रतिमा गड़ि मन्दिरे मन्दिरे।

त्वं हिं दुर्गा दशप्रहरणधारिणी
कमला कमल-दल-विहारिणी
वाणी विद्यादायिनी नमामि त्वां
नमामि कमलां अमलां अतुलाम्
सुजलां सुफलां मातरम्,
वन्दे मातरम्

श्यामलां सरलां सुस्मितां भूषिताम्
धरणीं भरणीम् मातरम्।।

Appendix III

INDEPENDENCE DAY PLEDGE

January 26, 1930

We believe that it is the inalienable right of the Indian people, as of any other people, to have freedom and to enjoy the fruits of their toil and have the necessities of life, so that they may have full opportunities of growth. We believe also that if any government deprives a people of these rights and oppresses them, the people have a further right to alter it or to abolish it. The British Government in India has not only deprived the Indian people of their freedom but has based itself on the exploitation of the masses, and has ruined India economically, politically, culturally, and spiritually. We believe, therefore, that India must sever the British connection and attain *Purna Swaraj* or complete independence.

India has been ruined economically. The revenue derived from our people is out of all proportion to our income. Our average income is seven pice (less than two pence) per day, and of the heavy taxes we pay, 20 per cent are raised from the land revenue derived from the peasantry and 3 per cent from the salt tax, which falls most heavily on the poor.

Village industries, such as hand-spinning, have been destroyed, leaving the peasantry idle for at least four months in the year, and dulling their intellect for want of handicrafts, and nothing has been substituted, as in other countries, for the crafts thus destroyed.

Customs and currency have been so manipulated as to heap further burdens on the peasantry. British manufactured goods constitute the bulk of our imports. Customs duties betray clear partiality for British manufactures, and revenue from them is used not to lessen the burden on the masses but for sustaining a highly extravagant administration. Still more arbitrary has been the manipulation of the exchange ratio which has resulted in millions being drained away from the country.

Politically, India's status has never been so reduced as under the British regime. No reforms have given real political power to the people. The tallest of us have to bend before foreign authority. The rights of free expression of opinion and free association have been denied to us, and many of our countrymen are compelled to live in exile abroad and cannot return to their homes. All administrative talent is killed, and the masses have to be satisfied with petty village offices and clerkships.

Culturally, the system of education has torn us from our moorings, and our training has made us hug the very chains that bind us.

Spiritually, compulsory disarmament has made us unmanly and the presence of an alien army of occupation, employed with deadly effect to crush in us the spirit of resistance, has made us think that we cannot look after ourselves or put up a defence against foreign aggression, or even defend our homes and families from the attacks of thieves, robbers, and miscreants.

We hold it to be a crime against man and God to submit any longer to a rule that has caused this fourfold disaster to our country. We recognise, however, that the most effective way of gaining our freedom is not through violence. We will therefore prepare ourselves by withdrawing, so far as we can, all voluntary association from the British Government, and will prepare for civil disobedience, including non-payment of taxes. We are convinced that if we can but withdraw our voluntary help and stop payment of taxes without doing violence, even under provocation, the end of this inhuman rule is assured. We therefore hereby solemnly resolve to carry out the Congress instructions issued from time to time for the purpose of establishing Purna Swaraj.

THE FLAG

A flag is a necessity for all nations. Millions have died for it. It is no doubt a kind of idolatry which it would be a sin to destroy. For, a flag represents an ideal. The unfurling of the Union Jack evokes in the English breast sentiments whose strength it is difficult to measure. The Stars and Stripes means a world to the Americans. The Star and the Crescent will call forth the best bravery of Islam.

It will be necessary for us Indians—Hindus, Muslims, Christians, Jews, Parsis, and all others to whom India is their home—to recognize a common flag to live and to die for.

— M.K. Gandhi

Origin

The evolution of the Indian National Flag reflects the political developments in the country among the 20th century. The various political trends, communal tensions, waves of enthusiasm can all be seen in the people's attitude to the flag.

The first national flag in India is said to have been hoisted on August 7, 1906, in the Parsee Bagan Square (Green Park) in Calcutta. The flag was composed of horizontal strips of red, yellow and green.

The red strip at the top had eight white lotuses embossed on it in a row. On the yellow strip the words *Vande Mataram* were inscribed in deep blue in *Devanagari* characters. The green strip had a white sun on the left and a white crescent and star on the right.

The second flag was hoisted in Paris by Madame Cama and her band of exiled revolutionaries in 1907 (according to some in 1905). This was very similar to the first flag except that the top strip had only one lotus but seven stars denoting the *Saptarishi*. This flag was also exhibited at a socialist conference in Berlin.

By the time our third flag went up in 1917, our political struggle had taken a definite turn. Dr. Annie Besant and Lokmanya Tilak hoisted it during the Home Rule Movement. This flag had five red and four green horizontal strips arranged alternately, with seven stars in the Saptarishi configuration super-imposed on them. In the left-hand top corner (the pole end) was the Union jack. There was also a white crescent and star in one corner.

This indicated the aspirations of the time. The inclusions of the Union Jack symbolised the goal of Dominion Status.

The presence of the Union Jack, however, made the flag generally unacceptable. The political compromise that it implied was not popular. The call for new leadership brought Mohandas Karamchand Gandhi to the fore in 1921 and, through him, the first tricolour. During the session of the All India Congress Committee which met at Bezwada (now Vijayawada) about this time, an Andhra youth prepared a flag and took it to Gandhiji. It was made up of two colours—red and green—representing the two major communities. Gandhiji suggested the addition of a white strip to represent the remaining communities of India and the *charkha* to symbolise progress.

Thus was the tricolour born, but it had not yet been officially accepted by the All India Congress Committee. Gandhiji's approval, however, made it sufficiently popular to be hoisted on all Congress occasions.

In 1931, when the A.I.C.C. met at Karachi, a resolution was passed stressing the need for a flag which would be officially acceptable to the Congress. There was already considerable controversy over the significance of the colours in the flag. Communal troubles had set in. The two major communities were at the parting of the ways and the stress was on communal interpretation.

Meanwhile a committee of seven was appointed to elicit opinion on the choice of a flag. It suggested a plain saffron flag with a *charkha* in reddish brown in the extreme left-hand corner. The A.I.C.C. did not accept the suggestion.

The year 1931 was a landmark in the history of the flag. A resolution was passed adopting a tricolor flag as our national flag. This flag, the forbear of the present one, was saffron, white and green. It was, however, clearly stated that it bore no communal significance and was to be interpreted thus:

Saffron for courage and sacrifice
White for truth and peace
Green for faith and chivalry

It also carried a *charkha* in blue on the white band. The size was three breadths by two breadths.

This resolution for the first time conferred official Congress recognition on the tricolour as the National Flag. Henceforward it became our Flag and the symbol of our determination to be free. On July, 22, 1947, the Constituent Assembly adopted it as Free India's National Flag. After the advent of Independence, the colours and their significance remained the same. Only the *Dharma Chakra* of Emperor Ashoka was adopted in place of the *charkha* as the emblem on the flag.

Adoption

On July 22, 1947, Shri Jawaharlal Nehru moved the following resolution in the Constituent Assembly:

> "Resolved that the National Flag of India shall be a horizontal tricolour of deep saffron (*Kesari*), white and dark green in equal proportions. In the centre of the white band there shall be a wheel in navy blue to represent the *charkha*. The design of the wheel shall be that of the wheel (*chakra*) which appears on the abacus of the Sarnath Lion Capital of Ashoka.
>
> "The diameter of the wheel shall be approximate to the width of the white band."

"The ratio of the width to the length of the flag shall ordinarily be two breadths by three breadths."

The above resolution was followed by a speech by the Prime Minister which ended all controversy about the interpretation of the flag. He said:

"I am sure that many in this House will feel the glow and warmth which I feel at the present moment, for behind this Resolution and the Flag which I have the honour to present to this House for adoption lies history, the concentrated history of a short span in a nation's existence. Sometimes in a brief period we pass through the track of centuries. . . . I remember the ups and downs of the great struggle for freedom of our great nation. I remember, and many in this House will remember, how we looked up to this Flag not only with pride and enthusiasm but with a tingling in our veins and also how, when we were sometimes down and out, the sight of this Flag gave us courage to go on. Many who are not present here today, many of our comrades who have passed, held on to this Flag, a few of them even unto death, and handed it over, as they sank, to other to hold it aloft. Therefore behind these simple words of the Resolution there is the struggle of the people for freedom with all its ups and downs, and trials and disasters, and a certain triumps—which I feel, in moving this Resolution—in the conclusion of that struggle. . . .

"It is a Flag which has been variously described. Some people, having misunderstood its significance, have thought of it in communal terms and believed that some part of it represents this community or that. But I may say that when this Flag was devised there was no communal significance attached to it. We thought of a design for a flag which was beautiful, because the symbol of a nation must be beautiful to look at. We thought of a flag which, in its combination and in its separate parts, would represent the spirit of the nation, the tradition of synthesis which has characterised us for thousands of years. . . .

"Now, Sir, may I say a few words about this particular

flag? It will be seen that there is a slight variation from the one many of us have used during these past years. The colours are the same deep saffron, a white and a dark green. In the white previously there was the *charkha* which symbolized the common man in India, which symbolized the masses of the people, which symbolized their industry and which came to us from the message which Mahatma Gandhi delivered. Now this particular *charkha* symbol has been slightly varied in this flag not taken away at all. Why has it been varied? Normally speaking, the symbol on one side of the flag should be exactly the same as on the other side. Otherwise, there is a difficulty which goes against the conventions. Now, the *charkha* as it appeared previously on this flag had the wheel on one side and the spindle on the other. If you see the other side of the flag, the spindle comes the other way and the wheel comes this way. There was this practical difficulty. Therefore, after considerable thought we were convinced that this great symbol which enthused the people should continue, but that it should continue in a slightly different form, that the wheel should be there and not the rest of the *charkha, i.e.,* the spindle and the string which created this confusion. The essential part of the *charkha* should there, that is, the wheel. So the old tradition continues in regard to the *charkha* and the wheel.

"But what type of wheel should we have? Our minds went back to many wheels but notably one famous wheel which had appeared in many places and which all of us have seen, the one at the top of the capital of the Ashoka column and in many other places. That wheel is a symbol of India's ancient culture, it is a symbol of the many things that India has stood for through the ages. We therefore thought that this wheel, this *chakra* emblem, should appear on our Flag. For my part, I am exceedingly happy that we have associated with our Flag not only this emblem but in a sense the name of Ashoka, one of the most magnificent names in India's history and the world. It is well that at this moment of strife, conflict and intolerance, our minds should go back towards what India stood for in the ancient days and what, I hope and believe, it has essentially stood for throughout the ages.

"Since I have mentioned the name of Ashoka I should like you to remember that the Ashoka period was essentially an international period of Indian history. It was not a narrowly national period. It was a period when India's ambassadors went abroad to far countries, not in the way of an empire and imperialism but as ambassadors of peace and culture and goodwill. Therefore this Flag that I have the honour to present to you is not, I hope and trust, a flag of empire, a flag of imperialism, a flag of domination over anybody, but a flag of freedom, not only for ourselves but to all people who may see it. And whatever it may go—and hope it will go far, not only where Indians dwell as our ambassadors and ministers but across the far seas where it may be carried by Indian ships—it will bring a message of friendship and comradeship, a message that India wants to befriend with every country of the world and that India wants to help any people who seek freedom."

Description

The flag presented by Shri Nehru to the Constituent Assembly was a tricolour rectangular panel, made up of three rectangular panels or sub-panels of equal width. The colour of the top panel is India Saffron (*kesari*) and of the bottom panel India Green. The middle panel is white, bearing in the centre the design of the Ashoka Chakra, in navy blue. The chakra should preferably be screen-printed on both sides of the flag, or otherwise printed, stencilled or suitably embroidered on both sides in all cases. The superimposed cloth must be of the same material as that of the body.

Besides the Prime Minister, Dr. Radhakrishnan and others in the Constituent Assembly stressed that the colours had no communal significance whatsoever.

Dr. Radhakrishnan interpreted the colours in philosophical terms. Bhagwa or saffron colours denotes renunciation specifications. On other occasions also, it is desirable that disinterestedness. Our leaders, he said, must be indifferent to material gains and dedicate themselves to their work. The white in the centre is light, the path of truth to guide our conduct. The green shows our relation to the soil, "our relation to the plant life here on which all other life depends."

The Ashoka wheel in the centre of the white is the wheel of the Law of Dharma. "Truth or Satya, dharma or virtue", Dr. Radhakrishnan said, "ought to be controlling principles of all those who work under this flag. Again, the wheel denotes motion. There is death in stagnation. There is life in movement. India should no more resist change, it must move and go forward. The wheel represents the dynamism of a peaceful change and hence this deviation does not revolt against the original idea of having a spinning wheel in the National flag."

Some historians trace the wheel even futher back than Ashoka's time. It was an old symbol of Buddhism. In fact some scholars trace it back to Hinduism. It occurs in the prehistoric sites in the Indies Valley. It was the solar symbol in Indian, Persian, early Egyptian, Assyrian and Greek religions. The wheel we have adopted on our national standard today has been known and revered by India and other countries for over 5,000 years.

Use

Every free country in the world has an elaborate and strict etiquette connected with the use of its National Flag. The best way to respect a country's flag is to learn and abide by the formalities regarding its use. The ceremonial attending the hoisting, lowering, saluting or half-masting of the flag must be adhered to by all institutions and individuals.

An equally important point is that the material, size and colours used in the flag are standardized. Nothing is so undignified or repugnant as a limp, discoloured or disproportionate Flag. At the request of the Ministry of Home Affairs and Army Headquarters, the Indian Standards Institutions has brought out an Indian Standard Specification which covers the essential requirements of the National Flag of India, and all Flags used for official display should conform to these only flags of appropriate sizes are used. Five standard sizes of the Flag, including those for cars, have been decided on, viz., 21' × 14', 18' × 12', 6' × 4', 12" × 8" and 9" × 6". The dyes, cloth and all other material needed for the Flag undergo rigid scientific tests. A sealed sample of the standard Flag is kept in the custody of the Indian Standards Institution. Arrangements for the manufacture and supply of the National Flag exist at the Ordnance Clothing Factory, Shahjahanpur.

Two of the Flag colours have been described as India Saffron and India Green. These colours did not occur in the standard colour-tables of the world. India Green and India Saffron being peculiar to the National Flag of India, have been scientifically determined by trichnomatic methods and accordingly defined in precise terms in Indian terms in Indian Colour Standard for the National Flag.

Our Flag has always been of hand-spun and hand-woven material and as the general sentiment of the people and of the Prime Minister, favoured this, the specifications were limited to cotton and hand-spun wool and silk.

Certain courtesies due to a national flag are recognized all over the world. India too has partly evolved, partly adopted, the tradition of correct usage with the Flag and to give the necessary etiquette legal sanction, the Government has laid down a "Flag Code—India."

Courtesy to National Flag

Wherever the Flag is flown, it shall occupy the position of honour and be distinctly placed.

When the Flag is flown on public buildings it shall be displayed on all days including Sundays and holidays from sun-rise to sun-set, irrespective of whether conditions. The Flag may be flown on the buildings at night also but only on very special occasions.

The Flag shall always be hoisted briskly and lowered slowly and ceremoniously. When accompanied by appropriate bugle calls, the hoisting and the lowering of the Flag should be simultaneous with the bugle calls.

When the Flag is displayed from a staff projecting horizontally or at an angle from a windowsill, balcony, or front of a building, the saffron side shall be at the farther end of the staff.

When it is displayed in a manner otherwise than by being flown from a staff, the saffron band must be uppermost when it is displayed flat and horizontal on a wall; when displayed vertically the saffron band should be to the left of a person standing facing it.

When displayed over the middle of a street, running east-west or north-south, the flag shall be suspended vertically with the saffron to the north, or to the east as the case may be.

If flown on a speaker's platform, the Flag shall be on the speaker's right. If otherwise displayed the Flag shall be above and behind the speaker.

When used on occasion like the unveiling of statue, the Flag shall be displayed distinctly and separately. It shall not be used as covering for the statue or monument.

When displayed on a motor car, the Flag shall be flown from a staff affixed firmly to the car, in the front.

When the Flag is carried in a procession or a parade, it shall be either on the marching right, that is the Flag's own right, or if there is a line of other flags, in front of the centre of the line.

Incorrect Display

A damaged or dishevelled Flag shall not be displayed, nor shall it be displayed or fastened, used or stored in any manner as may damage it.

The Flag shall not be dipped in salute to any person or thing. No other flag or bunting shall be placed higher or above the National Flag; nor shall any object including flowers or garlands or emblem placed on or above the Flag-mast from which the National Flag is flown.

The Flag shall not be used as festoon, rosette or bunting or in any other manner for decoration.

Appendix V

TEXT OF THE QUIT INDIA RESOLUTION ADOPTED ON 8 AUGUST, 1942

A meeting of the A.I.C.C. (All India Congress Committee) was held in Bombay on August 7 and 8, 1942. The following resolution recommended by the Working Committee was passed by an overwhelming majority, only 13 members dissenting.

Quit India

The All India Congress Committee has given the most careful consideration to the reference made to it by the Working Committee in their resolution dated July 14, 1942, and to subsequent events, including the development of the war situation, the utterances of responsible spokesmen of the British Government, and the comments and criticisms made in India and abroad. The Committee approves of and endorses that resolution and is of opinion that events subsequent to it have given it further justification, and have made it clear that the immediate ending of British rule in India is an urgent necessity, both for the sake of India and for the success of the cause of the United Nations. The continuation of that rule is degrading and enfeebling India and making her progressively less capable of defending herself and of contributing to the cause of world freedom.

The Committee had viewed with dismay the deterioration of the situation on the Russian and Chinese fronts and conveyed to the Russian and Chinese peoples its high appreciation of their heroism in defence of their freedom. This increasing peril makes it incumbent on all those who strive for freedom and who sympathise with the victims of aggression to examine the foundations of the policy so far pursued by the Allied Nations, which have led to repeated and disastrous failure. It is not by adhering to such aims and policies and methods that failure can be converted into success, for past experience has shown that failure is inherent in them. These policies have been based not on freedom so much as on the domination of subject and colonial countries, and the continuation of the imperialist tradition and method. The possession of empire, instead of adding to the strength of the ruling Power, has become a burden and a curse. India, the classic land of modern imperialism, has become the crux of the question, for by the freedom of India will Britain and the United Nations be judged, and the people of Asia and Africa be filled with hope and enthusiasm. The ending of British rule in this country is thus a vital and immediate issue on which depend the future of the war and the success of freedom and democracy. A free India will assure this success by throwing all her great resources in the struggle for freedom and against the aggression of nazism, fascism and imperialism. This will not only affect materially the fortunes of the war, but will bring all subject and oppressed humanity on the side of the United Nations, and give these Nations, whose ally India would be, the moral and spiritual leadership of the world. India in bondage will continue to be the symbol of British imperialism and the taint of that imperialism will affect the fortunes of all the United Nations.

The peril of today, therefore, necessitates the independence of India and the ending of British domination. No future promises or guarantees can affect the present situation or meet that peril. They cannot produce the needed psychological effect on the mind of the masses. Only the glow of freedom now can release that energy and enthusiasm of millions of people which will immediately transform the nature of the war.

The A.I.C.C. therefore repeats with all emphasis the demand for the withdrawal of the British Power from India. On declaration of India's independence, a Provisional Government will be formed and Free India will become an ally of the United Nations, sharing with them in the trials and tribu conlations of the joint enterprise of the struggle for freedom. The Provisional Government can only be formed by the co-operation of the principal parties and groups in the country. It will thus be a composite government representative of all important sections of the people of India. Its primary functions must be to defend India and resist aggression with all the armed as well as the non-violent forces at its command, together with its allied powers to promote the well-being and progress of the workers in the fields and factories and elsewhere to whom essentially all power and authority must belong. The Provisional Government will evolve a scheme for a Constituent Assembly which will prepare a constitution for the Government of India acceptable to all sections of the people. This constitution, according to the Congress view, should be a federal one, with the residuary powers vesting in these units. The future relations between India and the Allied Nations will be adjusted by representatives of all these free countries conferring together for their mutual advantage and for their co-operation in the common task of resisting aggression. Freedom will enable India to resist aggression effectively with the people's united will and strength behind it.

The freedom of India must be the symbol of and prelude to the freedom of all other Asiatic nations under foreign dominations. Burma, Malaya, Indo-China, the Dutch Indies, Iran and Iraq must also attain their complete freedom. It must be clearly understood that such of these countries as are under Japanese control now must not subsequently be placed under the rule or control of any other colonial Power.

While the A.I.C.C. must primarily be concerned with the independence and defence of India in this hour of danger, the Committee is of opinion that the future peace, security and ordered progress of the world demand a World Federation of free nations, and on no other basis can the problems of the modern world be solved. Such a World Federation would ensure the freedom of its constituent nations, the prevention of aggression and exploitation by one nation over another, the protection of national minorities, the advancement of all backward areas and peoples, and the pooling of the world's resources for the common good of all. On the establishment of such a World Federation, disarmament would be practicable in all countries, national armies, navies and air force would no longer be necessary, and a World Federal Defence Force would keep the world peace and prevent aggression.

An independent India would gladly join such a World Federation and co-operate on an equal basis with other nations in the solution of international problems.

Such a Federation should be open to all nations who agree with its fundamental principles. In view of the war, however, the Federation must inevitably, to begin with, be confined to the United Nations. Such a step taken now will have a most powerful effect on the war, on the peoples of the Axis countries, and on the peace to come.

The Committee regretfully realises, however, that despite the tragic and overwhelming lessons of the war and the perils that overhang the world, the governments of few countries are yet prepared to take this inevitable step towards World Federation. The reaction of the British Government and the misguided criticisms of the foreign press also make it clear that even the obvious demand for India's independence is resisted, though this has been made essentially to meet the present peril and to enable India to defend herself and help China and Russia in their hour of need. The Committee is anxious not to embarrass in any way the defence of China or Russia, whose freedom is precious and must be preserved, or to jeopardise the defensive capacity of the United Nations. But the peril grows both to India and these nations, and inaction and submission to a foreign administration at this stage is not only degrading India and reducing her capacity to defend herself and resist aggression, but is no answer to that growing peril and is no service to the peoples of the United Nations. The earnest appeal of the Working Committee to Great Britain and the United Nations has so far met with no response, and the criticisms made in many foreign quarters have shown an ignorance of India's and the world's need, and sometimes even hostility to India's freedom, which is significant of a mentality of domination and racial superiority which cannot be tolerated by a proud people conscious of their strength and of the justice of their cause.

The A.I.C.C. would yet again, at this last moment, in the interest of world freedom, renew this appeal to Britain and the United Nations. But the Committee feels that it is no longer justified in holding the nation back from endeavouring to assert its will against an imperialist and authoritarian government which dominates over it and prevents it from functioning in its own interest and in the interest of humanity. The Committee resolves, therefore, to sanction for the indication of India's inalienable right to freedom and independence, the starting of a mass struggle on non-violent lines on the widest possible scale, so that the country might utilise all the non-violent strength it has gathered during the last twenty-two years of peaceful struggle. Such a struggle must inevitably be under the leadership of Gandhiji and the Committee requests him to take the lead and guide the nation in the steps to be taken.

The Committee appeals to the people of India to face the dangers and hardships that will fall to their lot with courage and endurance, and to hold together under the leadership of Gandhiji, and carry out his instructions as disciplined soldiers of Indian freedom.

A NEW STAR RISES IN THE EAST

Pt. Nehru's Message to the Nation

The appointed day has come—the day appointed by destiny, and India stands forth again after long slumber and struggle, awake, vital, free and independent. The past clings on to us still in some measure and we have to do much before we redeem the pledges we have so often taken. Yet the turning point is past, history begins anew for us, the history which we shall live and act as others will write about.

It is a fateful moment for us in India, for all Asia and for the world. A new star rises, the star of freedom in the East, a new hope comes into being, a vision long cherished materialises. May the star never set and that hope never be betrayed.

We rejoice in that freedom, even though clouds surround us, and many of our people are sorrow stricken and difficult problems encompass us. But freedom brings responsibilities and burdens and we have to face them in the spirit of a free and disciplined people.

On this day our first thoughts go to the Architect of this freedom, the Father of our Nation who, embodying the old spirit of India, held aloft the torch of freedom and lighted up the darkness that surrounded us. We have often been unworthy followers of his and have strayed from his message, but not only we but succeeding generations will remember this message and bear the imprint in their hearts of this great son of India, magnificent in his faith and strength and courage and humility. We shall never allow that torch of freedom to be blown out however high the wind or stormy the tempest.

Our next thoughts must be of the unknown volunteers and soldiers of freedom who, without praise or reward, have served India even unto death.

We think also of our brothers and sisters who have been cut off from us by political boundaries and who unhappily cannot share at present in the freedom that has come. They are of us and will remain of us whatever may happen, and we shall be sharers in their good and ill fortune alike.

The future beckons to us whither do we go and what shall be our endeavour? To bring freedom and opportunity to the common man, to the peasants and workers of India. To fight and end poverty and ignorance and diseases. To build up a prosperous, democratic and progressive nation, and to create social, economic and political institutions which will ensure justice and fullness of life to every man and woman.

We have hard work ahead. There is no resting for any one of us till we redeem our pledge in full, till we make all the people of India what destiny intended them to be. We are citizens of a great country, on the verge of bold advance, and we have to live up to that high standard. All of us to whatever religion we may belong are equally the children of India with equal rights, privileges and obligations. We cannot encourage communalism or narrow-mindedness, for no nation can be great whose people are narrow in thought or in action.

To the nations and people of the world we send greetings and pledge ourselves to co-operate with them in furthering peace, freedom and democracy. And to India our much-loved motherland, the ancient, the eternal and the ever-new, we pay our reverent homage and we bind ourselves afresh to her service.

FIRST SERVANT OF THE INDIAN PEOPLE*

Fellow countrymen, it has been my privilege to serve India and the cause of India's freedom for many years. Today I address you for the first time officially as the First Servant of the Indian people, pledged to their service and their betterment. I am here because you willed it so and I remain here so long as you choose to honour me with your confidence.

We are a free and sovereign people today and we have rid ourselves of the burden of the past. We look at the world with clear and friendly eyes and at the future with faith and confidence.

The burden of foreign domination is done away with, but freedom brings its own responsibilities and burdens, and they can only be shouldered in the spirit of a free people, self-disciplined, and determined to preserve and enlarge that freedom.

We have achieved much; we have to achieve much more. Let us then address ourselves to our new tasks with the determination and adherence to high principles which our great leader has taught us. Gandhiji is fortunately with us to guide and inspire and ever to point out to us the path of high endeavour. He taught us long ago that ideals and objectives can never be divorced from the methods adopted to realize them; that worthy ends can only be achieved through worthy

* Jawaharlal Nehru's first broadcast to the nation as Prime Minister on August 15, 1947.

means. If we aim at the big things of life, if we dream of India as a great nation giving her age-old message of peace and freedom to others, then we have to be big ourselves and worthy children of Mother India. The eyes of the world are upon us watching this birth of freedom in the East and wondering what it means.

Our first and immediate objective must be to put an end to all internal strife and violence, which disfigure and degrade us and injure the cause of freedom. They come in the way of consideration of the great economic problems of the masses of the people which so urgently demand attention.

Our long subjection and the World War and its aftermath have made us inherit an accumulation of vital problems, and today our people lack food and clothing and other necessaries, and we are caught in a spiral of inflation and rising prices. We cannot solve these problems suddenly, but we cannot also delay their solution. So we must plan wisely so that the burdens on the masses may grow less and their standards of living go up. We wish ill to none, but it must be clearly understood that the interest of our long-suffering masses must come first and every entrenched interest that comes in their way must yield to them. We have to change rapidly our antiquared land tenure system, and we have also to promote industrialization on a large and balanced scale, so as to add to the wealth of the country, and thus to the national dividend which can be equitably distributed.

Production today is the first priority, and every attempt to hamper or lessen production is injuring the nation, and more especially harmful to our labouring masses. But production by itself is not enough, for this may lead to an even greater concentration of wealth in a few hands, which comes in the way of progress and which, in the context of today, produces instability and conflict. Therefore, fair and equitable distribution is essential for any solution of the problem.

The Government of India have in hand at present several vast schemes for developing river valleys by controlling the flow of rivers, building dams and reservoirs and irrigation works and developing hydro-electric power. These will lead to greater food production and to the growth of industry and to all-round development. These schemes are thus basic to all planning and we intend to complete them as rapidly as possible so that the masses may profit.

All this requires peaceful conditions and the co-operation of all concerned, and hard and continuous work. Let us then address ourselves to these great and worthy tasks and forget our mutual wrangling and conflicts. There is a time for quarrelling and there is a time for co-operative endeavour. There is a time for work and there is a time for play. Today, there is no time for quarrelling or overmuch play, unless we prove false to our country and our people. Today, we must co-operate with one another and work together, and work with right goodwill.

I should like to address a few words to our Services, civil and military. The old distinctions and differences are gone and today we are all free sons and daughters of India, proud of our country's freedom and joining together in our service of her. Our common allegiances is to India. In the difficult days ahead our Services and experts have a vital role to play and we invite them to do so as comrades in the service of India.

OUR NATIONAL ANTHEM

Janaganamana Adhinayak Jaya He

Jana gana mana adhinayaka jaya he
Bharata bhagya bidhata
Punjab, Sindhu, Gujarat Maratha
Dravida, Utkala Banga,
Vindhya, Himachal, Jamuna, Ganga,
Vichchala jaladhi taranga,
Taba Shubha name jage, taba Shubha ashisha mange,
gahe taba jaya gatha
Jana gana mangal dayaka, jaya he
Bharata bhagya bidhata
Jaya he, jaya he, jaya he, jaya, jaya, jaya, jaya he.
Aharaha tabo abhano pracharita suni tabo udara bani,
Hindu, Bhouddha, Shika, Jaina, Prashika, Musalmano,
Christani,
Purba paschima ashe
Tabo shinghasana pase
Prema haro haya gantha
Janagana mangalo dayaka jaya he Bharata bhagya bidhata
Jaya he, jaya he, jaya he, jaya, jaya, jaya jaya he.
Ratri pravatila udila Ravi Chabi Purba Udayagiri bhale
Gahe bihangama punna samirana nab jibana rasa dhale
Tabo karunaruna rage
Nidrita Bharata jage
Tabo charone nata matha
Jaya, jaya, jaya he, jayarajeswara Bharata bhagya bidhata
Jaya he, jaya he, jaya he, jaya, jaya, jaya he
Bharata bhagya bidhata.

(*Rabindranath Tagore*)

जय हिन्द

जनगणमन-अधिनायक जय हे भारत-भाग्यविधाता।
पंजाब सिंधु गुजरात मराठा, द्राविड उत्कल बंग।
विन्ध्य हिमाचल यमुना गंगा, उच्छल-जलधितरंग।
तव शुभ नामे जागे, तव शुभ आशिष मांगे
गाहे तव जय-गाथा।

जनगण-मंगलदायक जय हे भारत-भाग्यविधाता।
जय हे! जय हे! जय हे! जय जय जय जय हे!
अहरह तव आह्वान प्रचारित, शुनि तव उदार वाणी।
हिन्दु बौद्ध शीख जैन पारसिक, मुसलमान क्रिस्टानी।
पूरब पश्चिम आसे, तव सिंहासन पाशे।
प्रेमहार हय गाथा।

जनगण-ऐक्यविधायक जय हे भारत-भाग्यविधाता।
जय हे! जय हे! जय हे! जय जय जय जय हे!
पतन-अभ्युदय-बधुर पंथा युग-युग-धावित यात्री।
हे चिरसारथि! तव रथचक्रे मुखरित पथ दिनरात्री।
दारूण विप्लव माझे, तव शंखध्वनि बाजे।
संकट-दुःख-त्राता।

जनगण-पथपरिचायक जय हे भारत-भाग्यविधाता।
जय हे! जय हे! जय हे! जय जय जय जय हे!
घोर तिमिरघन निबिड निशीथे पीडित मूर्छित देशे।
जाग्रत छिल तव अविचल मंगल नतनयने अनिमेषे।
दुःस्वप्ने आतंके, रक्षा करिले अंके।
स्नेहमयी तुमि माता।

जनगण-दुःखत्रायक जय हे भारत-भाग्यविधाता।
जय हे! जय हे! जय हे! जय जय जय जय हे!
रात्रि प्रभातिल, उदिल रविच्छवि पूर्व-उदय-गिरि-भाले।
गाहे विहंगम, पुण्य समीरण नव-जीवन-रस ढाले।
तव करूणारूण रागे, निद्रित भारत जागे।
तव चरणे नत माथा।

जय जय जय हे जय राजेश्वर, भारत-भागयविधाता।
जय हे! जय हे! जय हे! जय जय जय जय हे!

रविन्द्रनाथ टैगोर

Guide to mankinds' heart, Architect of India's destiny! Let there be an awakening in thine name. Let all the country in its various parts from the Himalayas to the sea, from end to end wake up and under thy blessings.

Let the followers of various religions, let East and West unite in bonds of love in the shadow of Thy throne, and proclaim Thy name.

Let sleeping India wake into the dawn of a new life, in the light of Thy glory.

National Anthem

When the Constituent Assembly of India met on 24 January, 1950 in the Constitution Hall to sign the Constitution, its President, Dr. Rajendra Parsad, began the proceedings with a statement on the question of a National Anthem of India.

The composition consisting of the words and music known as 'Janaganamana' is the National Anthem of India subject to such alternation in the words as Government may authorise as occasion arises; and the song 'Vandemataram' which has played a historic part in the struggle for Indian freedom shall be honoured equally with 'Janaganamana' and shall have equal status with it.

After the members of the Assembly had signed the Constitution Shri Ananthasayanam Ayyangar asked the President if he would permit all members of the House to sing 'Janaganamana' and the President giving his assent, Shrimati Purnima Banerji with other members sang it for the first time after its formal adoption as our National Anthem.

This was, however, not the first time that 'Janaganamana' was sung in the Constituent Assembly. The proceedings of the historic session of the body at midnight of 14 August 1947 ended with this song although it was then sung only as a national song following 'Sare Jahan Se Achcha Hindustan Hamara'. The first item on the agenda for this session was the singing of 'Vandemataram.' In the two years and four months between that date and 24 January 1950 when it was officially declared to be the nation's anthem it was in practice used as such throughout the country. Soon after Independence the Union Cabinet decided that 'Janaganamana' should be provisionally recognised as India's National Anthem till a choice was formally made by the Constituent Assembly. This interim decision was taken after the Prime Minister of India, Jawaharlal Nehru had consulted the Provincial Governors and Premiers.

'Janaganamana' was composed by Rabindranath Tagore sometime towards the end of 1911 and was first sung that year at the second day's sitting of the twenty-sixth session of the Indian National Congress held in Calcutta under the presidentship of Pandit Bishan Narayan Dhar. The choir included Shri Amal Home and Srimati Chitralekha Devi, wife of a former Vice-Chancellor of this University. Reporting the proceedings of this session Amrita Bazar Patrika called 'Janaganamana' a 'song of benediction' and 'The Bengalee', a paper edited by Surendranath Banerjee who was one of the principal organizers of this session of the Congress, called it a 'partriotic song' and published an English version of it in its report.

The uniqueness of 'Janaganamana' as a national anthem is its integration of the patriotic feeling with a feeling for universal humanity. And if Rabindranath had any political philosophy its essence was a fine complex of nationalism and internationalism.

In 'Janaganamana' national ideals are integrated with the ideals of humanity and the march to freedom is made to keep step with humanity's march to its fulfilment. And yet the profoundly religious element in the whole conception is unmistakable. And it is present in all his national songs. In the song that he composed for the second session of the Indian National Congress in Calcutta in 1886 he speaks of the Mother calling her children to their task. In the song he wrote at the age of sixteen he addresses his country as Divine Mother. And the same spirit is to be found in songs like 'ebar tor mara gange ban esechhe 'jay ma' bale bhasha tari', and 'matrimandira-punya-angan kara mahojjvala aja he' and many others. What is striking about the religious element in 'Janaganamana' is that unlike Bakimchandra's 'Vandemataram' and Tagore's own 'Ayi bhuvanamanamohini' it does not hypostatize the country into a Divine Mother but presents it as a living human society moving towards the realization of its destiny under some Divine dispensation. It is a hymn celebrating the regeneration of the 'Janaganamana', the collective mind of a people in a cosmic process which the poet views as the working of a divine purpose in history.

Appendix IX

THE 15TH OF AUGUST, 1947

Sri Aurobindo's Message

August 15th, 1947 is the birthday of free India. It marks for her the end of an old era, the beginning of a new age. But we can also make it by our life and acts as a free nation an important date in a new age opening for the whole world, for the political, social, cultural and spiritual future of humanity.

August 15th is my own birthday and it is naturally gratifying to me that it should have assumed this vast significance. I take this coincidence, not as a fortuitous accident, but as the sanction and seal of the Divine Force that guides my steps on the work with which I began life, the beginning of its full fruition. Indeed, on this day I can watch almost all the world-movements which I hoped to see fulfilled in my lifetime, though then they looked like impracticable dreams, arriving at fruition or on their way to achievement. In all these movements free India may well play a large part and take a leading position.

The first of these dreams was a revolutionary movement which would create a free and united India. India today is free but she has not achieved unity. At one moment it almost seemed as if in the very act of liberation she would fall back into the chaos of separate States which preceded the British conquest. But fortunately it now seems probable that this danger will be averted and a large and powerful, though not yet a complete union will be established. Also, the wisely drastic policy of the Constituent Assembly has made it probable that the problem of the depressed classes will be solved without schism or fissure. But the old communal division into Hindus and Muslims seems now to have hardened into a permanent political division of the country. It is to be hoped that this settled fact will not be accepted as settled for ever or as anything more than a temporary expedient. For if it lasts, India may be seriously weakened, even crippled: civil strife may remain always possible, possible even a new invasion and foreign conquest. India's internal development and prosperity may be impeded, her position among the nations weakened, her destiny impaired or even frustrated. This must not be; the partition must go. Let us hope that that may come about naturally, by an increasing recognition of the necessity not only of peace and concord but of common action, by the practice of common action and the creation of means for that purpose. In this way unity may finally come about under whatever form—the exact form may have a pragmatic but not a fundamental importance. But by whatever means, in whatever way, the division must go; unity must will be achieved, for it is necessary for the greatness of India's future.

Another dream was for the resurgence and liberation of the peoples of Asia and her return to her great role in the progress of human civilisation. Asia has arisen; large parts are now quite free or are at this moment being liberated: its other still subject or partly subject parts are moving through whatever struggles towards freedom. Only a little has to be done and that will be done today or tomorrow. There India has her part to play and has begun to play it with an energy and ability which already indicate the measure of her possibilities and the place she can take in the council of the nations.

The third dream was a world-union forming the outer basis of a fairer, brighter and nobler life for all mankind. That unification of the human world is under way; there is an imperfect initiation organised but struggling against tremendous difficulties. But the momentum is there and it must inevitably increase and conquer. Hero too India has begun to play a prominent part and, if she can develop that larger statesmanship which is not limited by the present facts and immediate possibilities but looks into the future and brings it nearer, her presence may make all the difference between a slow and timid and a bold and swift development. A catastrophe may intervene and interrupt or destroy what is being done, but even then the final result is sure. For unification is a necessity of Nature, and inevitable movement. Its necessity for the nations is also clear, for without it the freedom of the small nations may be at any moment in peril and the life even of the large and powerful nations insecure. The unification is therefore to the interests of all, and only human imbecility and stupid selfishness can prevent it; but these cannot stand for ever against the necessity of Nature and the Divine Will. But an outward basis is not enough; there must grow up an international spirit and outlook, international forms and institutions must appear, perhaps such developments as dual or multilateral citizenship, willed intercharge or voluntary fusion of cultures. Nationalism will have fulfilled itself and lost its militancy and would no longer find these things incompatible with self-preservation and the integrality of its outlook. A new spirit of oneness will take hold of the human race.

Another dream, the spiritual gift of India to the world has already begun. India's spirituality is entering Europe and America in an ever increasing measure. That movement will grow; amid the disasters of the time more and more eyes are turning towards her with hope and there is even an increasing resort not only to her teachings, but to her psychic and spiritual practice.

The final dream was a step in evolution which would raise man to a higher and larger consciouness and begin the solution of the problems which have perplexed and vexed him since he first began to think and to dream of individual perfection and a perfect society. This is still a personal hope and an idea, and ideal which has begun to take hold both in India and in the West on forward-looking minds. The difficulties in the way are more formidable than in any other field of endeavour, but difficulties were made to be overcome and if the Supreme Will is there, they will be overcome. Hero too, if this evolution is to take place, since it must proceed through a growth of the spirit and the inner consciousness, the initiative can come from India and, although the scope must be universal, the central movement may be hers.

Such is the content which I put into this date of India's liberation; whether or how far this hope will be justified depends upon the new and free India.

Appendix X

LIST OF PRESIDENTS OF INDIAN NATIONAL CONGRESS

S. No.	Year	Place	President
1.	1885	Bombay	Mr. W.C. Bonnerjee
2.	1886	Calcutta	Shri Dadabhai Naoroji
3.	1887	Madras	Justice Badruddin Tayabji
4.	1888	Allahabad	Mr. George Yule
5.	1889	Bombay	Sir William Wedderburn
6.	1890	Calcutta	Sir Pherozeshah Mehta
7.	1891	Nagpur	Mr. P. Ananda Charlu
8.	1892	Allahabad	Mr. W.C. Bonnerjee
9.	1893	Lahore	Shri Dadabhai Nacroji
10.	1894	Madras	Sir Alfred Web, M.P.
11.	1895	Poona	Mr. Surendra Nath Banerjee
12.	1896	Calcutta	Mr. Behmat Ullah Sayani
13.	1897	Amravati	Mr. Sankaran Nair
14.	1898	Madras	Mr. Anand Mohan Bose
15.	1899	Lucknow	Mr. Romesh Chandra Dutt
16.	1900	Lahore	Mr. N.G. Chandaverkar
17.	1901	Calcutta	Mr. D.E. Wacha
18.	1902	Ahmedabad	Mr. Surendra Nath Banerjee
19.	1903	Madras	Mr. Lal Mohan Ghosh
20.	1904	Bombay	Sir Henry Cotton
21.	1905	Banaras	Sh. Gopal Krishna Gokhale
22.	1906	Calcutta	Sh. Dadabhai Naoroji
23.	1907-8	Surat	Dr. Rash Behari Ghosh
24.	1909	Lahore	Pt. Madan Mohan Malviya

25.	1910	Allahabad	Sir William Wedderburn
26.	1911	Calcutta	Mr. Bishan Narain Dar
27.	1912	Bankipur	Mr. R.N. Mudholkar
28.	1913	Karachi	Nawab Syed Mohammed
29.	1914	Madras	Mr. Bhupendra Nath Basu
30.	1915	Bombay	Sir Satyendra Nath Sinha *(After War raised to Peerage)*
31.	1916	Lucknow	Mr. Ambika Charan Mozumdar
32.	1917	Calcutta	Mrs. Annie Besant
33.	1918	Delhi	Pt. Madan Mohan Malviya
34.	1919	Amritsar	Pt. Motilal Nehru
35.	1920 (Spl.)	Calcutta	Lala Lajpat Rai
35.	1920	Nagpur	Mr. Vijayaraghavachariar
36.	1921	Ahmedabad	Hakim Ajmal Khan
37.	1922	Gaya	Mr. Chittranjan Das
38.	1923	Calcutta	Maulana Mohd. Ali
39.	1924	Belgaum	Mahatama Gandhi
40.	1925	Kanpur	Smt. Sarojini Naidu
41.	1926	Guahati	Shri Sriniwas Iyengar
42.	1927	Madras	Dr. M.A. Ansari
43.	1928	Calcutta	Pt. Motilal Nehru
44.	1929	Lahore	Pt. Jawaharlal Nehru
45.	1931	Karachi	Sardar Vallabhbhai Patel
46.	1932	Delhi	Seth Ranchod Das Amrit Lal
47.	1933	Calcutta	Mrs. Nallini Sen Gupta
48.	1934	Bombay	Dr. Rajendra Parsad
49.	1936	Lucknow	Pt. Jawaharlal Nehru
50.	1936	Faizpur	Pt. Jawaharlal Nehru
51.	1938	Haripur	Shri Subhash Chandra Bose
52.	1939	Tripuri	Shri Subhash Chandra Bose
53.	1940	Ramgarh	Maulana Abul Kalam Azad
54.	1946	Meerut	Acharya J.B. Kriplani